3rd Funniest Man in America

Mike G. Williams

presents

Turkey Soup for the Sarcastic Soul
Volume #3

Life Happens

from —
Darrell & Barb.
2020

Shut Up, Smile, and carry a Plunger!

Foreword by Ken Davis

**Part three of a four-volume trilogy
about life, love, and the
pursuit of the perfect Pizza!**

CC Books

www.christiancomedian.com

All scripture references have been quoted from the New MMB version (Mike's Memory Bible). As usual, we did this so we did not have to pay royalties to the NASB, NKJV, NLB, KJV, NRSV, NIV, NWT, NAACP, ACLU, AA, AAA, SWF, or any of the others. Of course we passed the saving directly on to you! So please feel free to use you own Bible to check the references for scriptural accuracy.

The offices of Mr. Williams are located in the back of a 1974 Pinto station wagon on concrete blocks somewhere north of Lakeland, Florida. Office hours are varied and rather random although he can be reached by contacting his wife and leaving a detailed message anytime around the diner hour. Some prefer to find him on the World Wide Web at www.christiancomedian.com where he frequently checks his email while surfing for great deals on E-bay! His phone number is unlisted and although he has registered with www.donotcall.gov, many people seem to have his number, so ask around. Your purchase of this book allows Mike to continue to remain free of the confines of clerking for a federal judge or possibly obtaining a degree in small motor mechanics by mail order.

Turkey Soup for the Sarcastic Soul #3
Life Happens—Shut up, Smile, and Always Carry a Plunger
Copyright © 2005 Mike G. Williams

All rights reserved

Text preparation and layout by Pine Hill Graphics, Eugene, OR
Cover Art by Mike G. Williams because he is too cheap to hire a professional
Photo by Bob's Bait, Tackle, and Photography, Frostproof, FL
Illustrations by Chapman Williams
Packaged by Pine Hill Graphics

ISBN-13: 978-1-933150-05-5
ISBN-10: 1-933150-05-X

Printed in the United States of America (we think)

This book is dedicated to my dearest Mother Jackie Williams.

Your life taught me to find joy in tough circumstances, to find laughter in the midst of pain, and love God till the end. I miss you.

And to my three children...

Dear Children,

I share these books with the world, but if I cannot teach you the lessons contained herein it has been for naught. I pray that God will give me the time needed to instill in you the lessons and values I have learned as a follower of God and student of His Holy Word. For me to be able to leave this world knowing that somehow the faith was imparted to you would make my life a success. My prayers are for you to find your own personal connection to God on this journey we call life.

Love, Dad

Other Books by and to be by Mike G. Williams

Night Lights and Other Things That Save Toes 1996

*In Case of Rapture This Car will Swerve as
my Mother-in-Law Takes the Wheel 1999*

Turkey Soup for the Sarcastic Soul #1 2001

*Turkey Soup for the Sarcastic Soul #2
For The even More Sarcastic Soul 2002*

*Turkey Soup for the Sarcastic Soul #3 Life Happens!
Shut up, Laugh, and Carry a Plunger 2005*

*Turkey Soup for the Sarcastic Soul #4
(Catchy subtitle to be named next week)*

Men are from Mars Because Women Killed the ones on Venus 2005

A New York Times Best Seller 2006

(There will be more I'm sure.
It's not like Mike has anything else to do!)

Thank you!

The largest thanks will always go to God who chose to love me and give His Son for my redemption. I stand humbled by His grace and mercy. I still fear You.

To my wife and family for sharing with me the time to type my thoughts out one finger at a time. To my children! To my parents James and Jackie Williams. To Joe Stowell and David Jerimiah my radio pastors. To James Robinson and Bob Coy my television pastors. To my friends, Ken, Janet, Doug, Tina, Mark, Kelli, Chris, Ashliegh, Rob, Laura, Dean, Susan. To all my fantastic agency. To my mentors—Frank and Irene Brower, Bernard Okeke, John and Stelene Taylor, George and Jeanie DeTellis, Jack and Debby Peters, the Canines, the Overholts, Steve Smith, Robert Herrington, Ken Davis.

To the others—To those of you who purchased this book. To those of you across the country who have allowed me to ramble on their stages. To the CPC's hat have allowed me to share my gift with their groups. To the public schools who have let me speak to their students. Max Lucado, Eugene Peterson, Chuck Colson, Bill Gaither, Gloria Gaither, Jack Taylor, Robert Fulgham, and so many more.

To the other others—T.J. Foltz, Conan O'brien, Jay Leno, David Letterman, Carrot Top, Scot Thompson, Robert G. Lee, Tim Hawkins, Paul Aldrich, Nazareth, Gordon Douglas, Daren Streblow, Leeland Klassen, Justin Fennell, Thor Ramsey, Mike Warnke, Chonda Pierce, Mark Lowry, David Dean, Cecile Kaiser, Emo Phillips, Slappy Clark, Paul and Nicole Johnson, Michael Card, Brian Scheer, and the Carlton Gang.

And of course—To the cruise lines who have paid me to take vacations with my family. To Chuck E. Cheeses and Toys-R-Us. To the Waffle House and Denny's waitresses who make me feel thankful to have my job. To all the plumbers who have learned to carry a plunger long before this book was printed. To those who have ever owned a 1974 Ford Pinto, you know why! And to McNair Wilson who taught me how to cast out demons with a light overhand fly rod.

Editing thanks—In an effort to improve the grammar of this Turkey Soup volume 3, I asked the senior English class of Riverside Christian School in Yakima, Washington, to be the editors of this book. For their work I am very truly grateful. If you don't like the spelling or grammar in this one…blame them!

One more thing, Of course I want to thank *The Academy*. Whether or not I win, it has been an honor being nominated.

Of course He's not safe—He's a lion—but He is good!

C.S. Lewis

Foreword

by Ken Davis

In grade school there was a part of my report card designed to show social adjustment and personal normality. This was separate from the grades you received for math and reading. This was all about how you were proceeding as a human being. In this section of the card was a list of things like, works well with others, practices good hygiene, uses common sense, you get the idea. After each item in the list was a blank space where the teacher could write an "S" meaning satisfactory or a "U" meaning unsatisfactory.

I don't think Mike Williams did very well on this part of his report card. There is very little about Mike that is normal. Mike certainly would have gotten an "S" for sarcasm, but that was not included in the list. He would also have gotten an "S" for heart, because there are few people in the world with a bigger heart than Mike Williams. But heart wasn't on the list either.

Mike isn't like all the other children. He is very-very special. That uniqueness is perfectly demonstrated in Turkey Soup for the Sarcastic Soul Volume 3 (*plunger edition*). The wild sense of humor that got him in trouble at school, now creates a demand for appearances all over the world. It's in the book. The heart that enables him to use that humor to touch your soul still beats inside that huge gangly body. And it's in the book. I've read each one of Mike's books. This is the best. Mike is becoming ever more confident in how God made him, WEIRD! And he is becoming ever more articulate in using that gift to hammer home life changing truth.

Put on your seat belt and brace yourself. Here comes Turkey Soup for the Sarcastic Soul Volume 3.

Ken Davis
Communicator, Author, Comedian

Introduction

*W*elcome to volume three of this four-volume Turkey Soup for the Sarcastic Soul trilogy, the world's only known four-volume trilogy. I subtitled this book Life Happens—So Shut Up, Smile, and Carry a Plunger! It has nothing to do with the book, but it is a reminder to me that the humorous times in my memory banks are not remembrances of perfect days; they are memories of *imperfect* days. These were days when everything went wrong, the picnic where the ants ate my lunch before I did, the flat tires on the freeway, and sermons that I unknowingly preached with my *zipper* down. They are memories of the time my dog excitedly jumped off the porch to lovingly greet me and forgot that he was choker-chained to the wall. I will miss that dog! These are recollections of the wedding ceremony where I introduced the newlywed couple with the wrong last name... the last name of her *former* husband.

The stories that come up around our table often involve me falling into a grave while delivering a funeral eulogy. For you it may be the day you worked an entire afternoon with your skirt tucked in the back of your pantyhose. *Hopefully the men have never had that happen!* These are the days that have become fond memories, although they were not very fond as we were living them. Wouldn't it be great if we could learn to laugh while these *plunger days* were happening? You better believe it!

In this book I hope you laugh and I hope you learn. Most importantly, I hope you don't return this book to where you purchased it. I have already spent the publishers' advance. So, for the love of family, friends, and my mortgage, please keep it! Who knows, it may grow on you? *Like a virus.* Hey, life happens—shut up, smile, and carry a plunger!

To the King, to the Kingdom,
Mike G. Williams

Behind Every Rat
There Is a Tail

People always warn children about the dangers of running with scissors. They never warn them about running with hedge trimmers... I think that is where the real danger is.

Mike G. Williams

*W*e sat around the campfire telling our favorite frightening stories to the children before we put them to bed. I don't know just why. Maybe it is simply what males do. During my little fictional stroll down Mystery Science Theater lane, my son, Chapman, let out an enormously loud belch, which he and his little buddies found quite amusing. *It was a big one!* I have to say that as a father I was a bit proud! "That's my boy... belching like a full-grown man!" He did follow it up with a polite, albeit— obligatory, "Excuse me," but his pardon request came after his mother reminded him that he had "forgotten" something. She has had to remind me from time to time about the same thing. I'm rather forgetful!

I can't help but think that it is almost hypocritical to say "excuse me" after burping, if you knew you were going to burp. It certainly would be the expected norm to say it if you burped accidentally, in the middle of a wedding ceremony, or a eulogy, of course. But... to apologize after a pre-meditated, self-mustered, voluminous, pride-filled, bellowing release of air seems tantamount to lying. It's like stomping on a Mustard packet at a restaurant and saying, "I'm sorry, I didn't know it would explode all over your shoe lady!" It's like bringing your miniature poodle onto a neighbor's rug and saying, "Oops, I didn't think little Foo Foo would pee on your carpet like she does every *stinking* day on mine." It's like…well…you get the point.

"Excuse me" is a weak substitution for an apology. It is the "woops," the "I didn't mean to do that, or at least, didn't mean to get caught doing that," and the "uh-oh, sorry." Often it is almost a slap in the face to an actual apology. After I pointed this incongruity out to my beloved wife, she sarcastically suggested that I find a more appropriate statement, or at least, one that expressed what I felt should be said in place of this age-old standard. I fired back a few additions to the excuse me phrase, all of which made the burp itself seem quite tame. She rejected them all. She suggested that my flippant attitude toward pre-meditated, self-mustered, voluminous displays of bodily functions could only be interpreted as, "I don't give a rat's behind about my guests and obviously have no manners." *Hmmm, now there is an idea.* It was at that point in the evening that I started following each burp with her suggestion, and added another simple phrase to make it more personalized; for I wouldn't want to be outdone by a rank amateur. So, yes, as we sat there drinking *warmish* Coca Cola around the fire, I found multiple occasions to blurt, "I don't give a rat's behind about you or your uppity etiquette!" It got to the point where the entire group would join me in this mantra. Before long everyone, except my wife, was freeing themselves of carbon dioxide, *(at least, I think that is what they put in the Coca Cola)* and then shouting, "I don't give a rat's behind about you or your uppity etiquette!"

> I take exception to the label "hypochondriac." I prefer to think of myself as spectacularly self-absorbed.
>
> *Dennis Miller*

My little experiment (if you want to call it that) in human behavior brought to light a real problem: the average person's ability to truly apologize and the ability to take action to change. Some of you are not going to like what I am about to say, and some of you are going to be offended by my future use of the word *Yuppie*. Many will feel that it is inappropriate to identify a people group, especially if it hits too close to their *yuppiefied* demographic. If you are one of those who are offended by my words, I offer my sincerest, "Please excuse me!" Of course, you know what that means! I actually fall into that Yuppie age group myself.

A professional, licensed counselor-friend confessed to me that he felt that counseling Yuppies was often a total waste of time. He believed that most of them were nothing more than egomaniacal, self-serving, narcissistic, psychological hypochondriacs. He believed they were egomaniacal because they want nothing more than to be counseled so they could publicly further the implication that they really wanted to be a whole person, although they secretly only wanted their peers to admire them for having the courage to address their own spiritual or emotional well being. They were narcissistic because they loved the personal attention they personally received from not being left out of the ability to personally say, "My personal therapist said… Blah, blah, blah…" He referred to them as self-serving, because they continually tried to impress him with the way they desired a change or growth. He called them psychological hypochondriacs because they live to find another problem on which to blame their "ills." Does that sound like anyone you know? *Somebody get me a mirror!* My friend might have said more, but I wasn't paying attention to him; I was *thinking about myself.* I'm sure he didn't mean to implicate me in anyway.

Yes, there have been times when I let a person counsel me just for the sheer satisfaction of letting that person and others know how much I care about my spiritual health. That is unfortunately the awful truth. I would like to make you think more highly of me, but hey, here I

> You can win the rat race and still be a rat.
> *Stuart Little*

am, the man with more baggage than Samsonite! I think it was Dennis Miller who said, "I want to be thought of as the guy who couldn't care less if anybody thinks about him." *Don't take those quotation marks too seriously; I can't remember exactly, but that is a point well taken.* We all have an image to protect, even if that image is the image of a person who appears to not care about his image. Man that is deep! Well, deep for me. Did you wonder if I really meant that last sentence, or did you wonder if it was merely the image of deepness that I wanted you to perceive from me?

There comes a time in every person's life when they have to get real with themselves. A time when they will be forced have to look their own self in the face and ask the hard questions. The questions that make us all investigate the truth of our *stated desire* to be real Disciples of Christ. If there was such a thing as a *Disciples of Christ test,* how many of us would pass? I wonder if I would pass. Is there a GED available? How many tries do I get? Can I use my notes? *Do I get extra credit for my award-winning smile?* I certainly want people to believe that I am working hard in the *follow-ship* area. When I do make a mistake, or get caught in a mistake, I quickly blurt, "Excuse me!" Yeah, "excuse me," like I didn't mean to do it.

Sure! Most of the time "Excuse me" is simply the most expected thing to say. It is Brittany singing, "Woops I Did It Again." It is an apathetic apology from Archie Bunker. It is the "whatever!" It's nothing. There is no a real penance involved, or repentance, for that matter. Just another "excuse me." *Need I remind you what that means?*

> If we don't identify tempting thoughts and take them captive to what we know to be true—if we don't immediately replace the wrong thinking with the right thinking—we'll become so weak that we won't care what we do until after we've sinned and begun to taste the bitter consequences.
>
> *Gary J. Oliver*

We (you and I) need to guard ourselves against the pressure to perform phony penance for the impression of man, and turn our true penance toward the impression of God. Excuse me if that statement bothers you. Excuse me if that statement is not really clear. Let me try again. I need to quit exercising *phony repentance* in my life and truly come to a change of heart. I need to forget my need to justify or nullify my actions and concern myself with the judgment of an Almighty God. Despite my sarcasm, I truly do *give a rat's behind* about what you think. That unfortunately is one of my greatest problems. Pray for me, and I will pray for you. Pray that I will think less of man's opinions and more of God. May we all be willing to participate in heartfelt repentance. May we all learn that it is good and right to be truly sorry! An apology connected with a change brings about spiritual health.

Repent, change your current way of thinking, for it will not be long before the kingdom of heaven will be at your doorstep.
Matthew 3:2

I Didn't Know We Had to Report Serial Killers to the Police

I'm in the Jehovah Witness Protection Program. Nobody has knocked on my door in years.

Daren Streblow

J had just returned from LA and crawled into the bed to try and get some sleep. Now, of course, when I say "LA" I mean Los Angeles, and not *Lower* Alabama. The television was on channel ten; my wife was watching the news. There was Reginald Roundtree and Sue Zelinko reading to us the top stories of the day. There was a problem, however! An obnoxious red background had replaced the beautiful blue background that once was their set. It really jumped out at me. It screamed, "I am big and red! See the power of red! Fear the power of red!" I said to my wife, "What in the world is Channel Ten doing with that background? It's unnerving. I need a TUMS now!"

The very next night I found myself sitting next to Reginald Roundtree at a fundraising banquet for the *Kimberly Home*, a care center for women in crisis. I turned to him and poised a pertinent question. "So, Mr. Roundtree, what is up with the red? Was there a sale at Home Depot on red paint?" He explained that every other news station had a warm blue, and the owners were looking for a way to make Channel Ten stand out. Well, they accomplished the desire. According to Mr. Roundtree the decision was not without complaint from their senior audience. Our conversation moved to the latest conspiracy theory racing through the Capitol. We discussed the various websites that spout every kind of alternative explanation to anything that goes wrong. We even went as far as to discuss the Kennedy assassination. I explained that I had the chance to visit the Book Depository in Dallas, which now houses the Assassination Museum. I noted that I thought it must have been named after the infamous assassination took place. *I really don't think the CIA or the FBI would have named it that before the event.* I described for him the room that has been perfectly preserved, as it was that fateful day, *including the absence of Oswald!* That is just my opinion...and the opinion of Jimmy Hoffa, Adam Sandler, Martha Stewart, Tony the Tiger, and the dissenting members of the Warren Commission. I wanted to pole my good friends, Dr. Jeremiah and Dr. Stowell, on the issue but neither would accept my calls. I believe their response was, "Mike who?"

> You know you are getting older when you are watching the History Channel and you can remember when the event being depicted was not history—it was the news!
>
> *Mike G. Williams*

Reginald and I chatted for a few minutes longer, and just before I was able to ask my real question, he had to get back to the station to do the late news. *He explained that he was being paged, but I think he was just really bored.* The real question I wanted to eloquently pose to the man was, "What's up with the neighbors of serial killers nowadays? In an age of mutual distrust and conspiracy theories, why doesn't anybody suspect anything?" When the news interviews these neighborhood people (where a serial killer is found to have lived), they all say the same thing. "I never suspected a thing!" There is always someone who says, "He seemed like a really nice family man who just kept to himself." How can this be? In an age of publicized conspiracy beliefs and the wonderful movie *The Pelican Brief*, how can this really be? How can we not be suspicious of anybody other than ourselves? *I mean seriously, I personally think that all of my neighbors are weird and have been covertly placed there by the CIA to spy on me and report on all my stuff to headquarters.* Wherever that may be! I believe that my *Italian neighbors* across the street are in the Witness Protection Program. I'm not paranoid, of course! We put foil over all the windows so they can't see in, and we only talk in code with the radio turned up really loud. I wouldn't want them to hear what I want for supper. So there!

Let me digress a moment. Why can't they find at least one neighbor who says, "Yeah, I always knew there was something wrong with that dude.

They way he kept walking up and down the street screaming and drooling as he sharpened his twin blade bludgeoning axe, all the while whispering to his axe, and then urinating on the sidewalk before he went into the gun shop. I always knew he was a wacko—I just didn't know who to call." I understand that! You can't just call 9-1-1 and tell them that there is a weird one out here that really needs investigation. There is nobody to call. They should probably establish a special force team to investigate inner-neighborhood weirdness. No, that would be stereotyping people who were being weird. I'm sure the Civil Liberties Union would be all over that. Yes, them and their stereotypically weird attorneys. I don't mean that in a bad way.

> I love to sleep...
> I have dreams about
> taking naps!
>
> *Thor Ramsey*

Who can we call for weird, wacko, or suspicious? What number can you dial? In the airport they broadcast an announcement regarding seeing anything suspicious. They tell you to report any suspicious person to the nearest law enforcement agent. I often enjoy going up to an airport policeman and whispering, "See that lady over there with the cat in the pet carrier? No, don't look! She might see you! I think she is a suspicious person." If I take the announcement seriously about reporting suspicious persons to the police, I would have to report myself because I am a very suspicious person. I am suspicious about everybody. I should report myself to somebody. *I should call in a report of a possible axe murderer- me. I do own an axe!* There are very few things that, given the right circumstances, I am not capable of. Inside of me there is this evil fallen angel that keeps talking in my head. He is telling me to do bad things. He often convinces me that bad is really good. He explains that everybody else is doing it. He declares that nobody will

> We are not sinners
> because we sin; we sin
> because we are sinners.
>
> *R. C. Sproul*

ever find out. *He gives me neat, specific plans on burying my wife's body in an undetectable location.* I must quit listening to him! I must lean toward the Voice that beckons me to righteousness and peace, the voice that encourages me to do the godly things. It's a regular *schizophrenic world* up here in the cranial headquarters at times, but I must be careful. You should be careful too! I'm watching you. *I'm listening in at your house on my secret satellite eavesdropping devices right now as you read.*

There is a war going on in our minds. The things we should do, we don't do; and the things we should not do, we do. We must learn to delight ourselves in God's law to see spiritual and mental victory. We need the help of God to save us from our own demise. He will help us!

A short adaptation from Romans 7

Big Bad Bob!

*B*efore I met my father-in-law, I was warned about him. He stood six foot seven inches tall and looked meaner than a snake. He was actually a real puppy-dog, but he had an interesting, almost scowling, facial sculpture. He was also an Independent Fundamentalist Baptist preacher! *That really says enough, doesn't it?* I was also told that he had a great sense of humor and really loved to laugh. So… in an effort to get on, what I thought was, his good humor side, I decided to have a little fun with him. You know… break the ice. The Tuesday afternoon before I was supposed to meet the family and have dinner with them, I decided to have a pre-dinner rendezvous with the big Reverend. He didn't have any idea that one day he would be giving his daughter to me in marriage.

I never had much going for me in the early years, and things have *not changed that much* either! I was not rich. I was not smart. I was not handsome. I didn't come from a well-connected family. I was just Mike, the guy who drove a former Colorado Beef van. *Let me say that fathers just love to send their daughters off with men driving vans.* Therefore, in an effort to make a good impression on him with my only real talent, humor, I set off with an elaborate plan. This was a plan that would surely go down in history as the greatest practical joke ever played at the

Herrington house. At least, my dear Terica thought this would be a great plan.

Terica had told me that her father always went home and studied on Tuesday afternoon, and that he had been doing a study on Religious Cults Operating in North America. I stealthily drove past my local barbershop, and *borrowed* a few copies of the *Watchtower Magazine* from his rack. This is a magazine that is published by the Jehovah Witnesses. They are sure to be on his list of cults! Hey, for an Independent Fundamentalist Baptist, even the Methodists are on that list! With Watchtower magazines in my back pocket, I knocked on his door that fateful afternoon. His towering torso loomed ominously in the doorway as I smiled and said, "Hello Sir, I'm from the Colorado Beef Company, and you can purchase twenty of our finest steaks for only twenty dollars." After a quick rejection of the steaks, he explained that he was a minister and would love to tell me

> I don't want to be a Jehovah's Witness; I want to be a Jehovah's bystander.
> *Flip Wilson*

about how I could get eternal life for free. There was the bait! I told him I was a Jehovah Witness as I pulled a magazine out of my back pocket. He bought it, hook, line, and sinker!

We bantered back and forth about beliefs. As he would carefully explain what he believed, I would respond with, "I don't believe that!" I had very little idea what the Witnesses believed at that time. Looking back on what I said, I think my doctrine was more *Muslim-ish* than *Witness-ish*; however, I kept sticking to the fact that he needed to join the Watchtower Society in order to be assured that he and his family belonged in the chosen one-hundred and forty-four-thousand. I think I even quoted Buddha a few times to confuse the issues. I also told him that, as a pastor, he would probably be *grand-fathered* into a higher level than the rest of us, and because of that, I would be able to give him a special volume discount on the steaks. We talked outside of the door, because a true Independent Fundamentalist Baptist would never let a Witness actually come into their home. Apparently the doorstep was technically okay. *I sure hope they never need a plumber and he turns out to be a JW and secretly hides a Watchtower under the sink!* Sixty-five minutes later we parted ways with a common, "I will pray for you," and I headed back to the street to retrieve my van.

Three hours later I drove my van up their driveway and walked the steps to the house. My dearest Terica opened the door and winked as I sat down on the couch. It was but a matter of minutes before she brought her dad into the living room to meet me. I will never forget the look of *sheer horror* that crossed his face when he thought that his precious daughter was dating a *Witness*. I looked him in the face, stuck out my hand and said, "Hi, I'm Mike! I'm from the People Whose Daughters Think It Would Be Funny To Pull A Prank On Their Dad Society!" Yeah, I made sure he understood that she had something to do with it. He broke down and cried, we all laughed, and then we explained the little prank to the rest of the family.

Have you ever been suckered? Infomercial-ed? Snookered big-time? Ever gone after something hook, line, and sinker, only to find out it was a mirage? Yeah, me too! *If I only had a dollar for every time I called that 800 number and purchased the New and Improved Thigh Master, I would be a richer man today.* It's easy to get suckered. There are con men and women all over the place. Many operate under the guise of religion. This is why it is so important for us to know the inspired Word of God for ourselves If dear old Dad had not been biblically literate, I'll bet I could have used my salesmanship ability to sign him up for a magazine subscription.

Are you prepared to give defense for your beliefs when I knock on your door with a box of steaks? Or could I come to your door, a wolf in Witness clothing, and gain entrance? You may say "no," but what if I knocked on your door via the television screen. It happens almost every night with television shows and movies that we allow to lambaste our minds with *stinkin' thinkin'*. It happens as we allow the sexually-explicit shows about modern dating to get us primed to alter our moral behavior. Let's be honest, before we know it, we are mentally cheering for these sexual deviants to *get it on*. We must be careful. We must guard the doorstep of our minds and hearts... and those of our families. Don't tell me it can't happen to you. You are not that different from me. Well, *you may be thinner*, but that is not what I'm referring to, and you know it.

> I lost 120 pounds! People say you can see it in my face. In my face? What was I, the stinking Kool-Aide man?
> *John Pinette*

Guard your minds! Guard the gates of your palace. I believe it was Abraham Lincoln who once said, "No enemy will ever take this country from an invasion of our borders... Our enemy will only take us from within..." He went on to say more, and say it more eloquently than I

> It is hard to fight an enemy who has outpost in your head.
>
> *Sally Kempton*

quoted, but I think you get the point. We can bar the door, but if we leave open the windows, the thieves will still come in. We can lock the windows, but the invaders can still come through an unrestricted fireplace. Make sure your mental firewall is up and working! Study the Word! Know the Word! Fill your mind with the Word of God so you will not be deceived by the enemy.

Guard the vulnerable places like your heart and mind. Lock the door! Don't even answer the bell of the enemy. Pretend you're not at home.
1 Peter 1:13

Okay, One More Boat Story!

My mom use to say, "It won't be funny when that stick flies into somebody's eye!" Usually she was right... but that particular day we were playing a game called Throw a Stick into Somebody's Eye and Laugh! Mom is not always right.

Mike G. Williams

My friend Ken purchased a boat. A big boat! Forty feet long and fourteen feet wide! A houseboat!

A double-decker with two bedrooms, two helms, two engines, four anchors, and a whopping big generator! Now, my friend Ken is not a boat person! Boats require a "hands-on" mentality, and Ken is a "managerial" type. He is great at spouting out orders, but at sea those orders will serve quite useless with no deck hands. He needed someone who could maintain the boat for him. Ken could steer it rather well, but lowering the anchors, casting off lines, hoisting the sails, tying knots, and maintaining the multiple engines while hanging upside down through a small steel door, was not his forte. So…we became partners. It was a good deal for me. He put up the thousands of dollars, and I kept the twin Chrysler 318's and the generator in working order. I have some experience working on marine equipment, and the cost of repairing those things can be very expensive, not to mention, the time required to get an appointment at a large marine shop. Therefore, although I got a good deal—he did too.

For five years, along with our families, we cruised the boat on Lake Harris. Almost every Saturday, Ken and his wife cooked the steaks, and I hung upside down over the engine compartment. The twin Chrysler 318's were not equipped with electronic ignition. They were the old, point-style ignition that required gap gauges, and a dwell meter. You mechanic-types will understand what I'm saying. Because of all the moisture, they would have to be filed and adjusted almost every week. Usually, in a matter of two hours or so, we were ready to cruise the chain of lakes. So Ken would shout a few random nautical terms, none of which he actually understood, and I would untie us from the dock.

After a few years it became evident that our boat was going to need the bottom refinished. On a small boat refinishing is simply a matter of trailering the boat and painting it with some anti-fouling bottom paint. On a forty-foot, steel hulled cruiser, however, refinishing requires a sandblaster, welding torch, a 40- ton lift, and a dry dock. You have seen those big boat yards before, I'm sure. The decision was made that we would take the boat up to the boatyard in Jacksonville. This decision presented us with the initial problem.

> You're getting a little fat when you step on the bathroom scale, and you see a picture of John Candy waving to you.
> *Colin Quinn*

The trip from Lake Harris to Jacksonville takes four to five days and requires navigating some of the narrowest rivers in Florida. It requires bringing scuba equipment to enter the gator-infested water to untangle debris from the big brass props if needed. It requires bringing a chainsaw to cut limbs that are hanging too low to allow the boat to pass. It requires bringing enough food for the entire trip, unless eating at the two rickety fish camps along the way is at all appealing to you. Getting fuel at these places is okay, but make sure you are well armed. The problem was that my touring schedule did not allow a full week absence. I'm not saying that my being there would have made the trip a pleasure-cruise. Rather, I am saying that, as you will remember, I am the maintenance guy in this duo! Ken, however, decided that he could do it all by himself. Hey, he is the Captain!

My buddy set off on the adventure of a lifetime with fifty pounds of steak and lobster, eight cases of diet Mountain Dew, two hundred gallons of fuel, a cell phone, and a newly purchased captain's hat. He started his quest early Monday morning and, at the last minute, decided to bring his brother along for company. They were doing really well for the first two days! Ken cooked the food and shouted orders, as Steve worked the chainsaw. The problem happened on the third day of travel up the "environmentally protected" Ocklawaha River. Ken was broiling lobster, instead of watching the depth gauge, when they heard a low- pitched scraping sound. They had driven the boat over a huge cypress knee. The boat came to an abrupt stop. They could not go forward; they could not go backward. Marine protocol would have been to suit up, dive under the boat (in this darkest of water), and cut the cypress knee with a handsaw. *Chainsaws do not work underwater.* Neither of them possessed the required "macho-ness" to dive into these gator infested waters, so they continued to race the engines forward and backwards. *Where is the Crocodile Hunter when you really need him?* They were rocking the boat back and forth, hoping to break the cypress knee. If you know anything about cypress knees, you know that this isn't a real hopeful possibility! Yet, as real men, they tried and tried. Surprisingly enough, after about two-hours of this repetition (including a short pause for the consumption of lobster), they were successful. Down the river they went, their delay only costing them a couple of dozen gallons of fuel for their effort.

In the not-very-distant future, they began to notice that the boat was running a bit slower. No problem, give it a little more gas, right? That was always Ken's answer for any crisis. Around five that evening they began to notice that the bow (front) was sitting very low in the water. Hmmm… that's odd; give it some more gas! Within minutes the boat was riding so low in the water that the engines would no longer push the boat forward. This should have been a clear indication that they should check for a problem, which they did. Ken told Steve to open up the bow deck hatch and take a look. "Hey, is there supposed to be water in here?" Ken, break-ing with tradition, moved his captain's chair and began prying open the hatch below his feet. When he did so, water began to flow into the main cabin. *Houston, we have a problem here!* I can hear the theme from Gilligan's Island playing softly about now.

> Can you imagine what it would be like if Rodney Dangerfield came out as a Christian? "I tell you I don't get no respect. I went to get baptized. The preacher held me under!!!"
>
> *Danny Murphy*

It seems that during the back and forth motion of their cypress knee ordeal, they had inadvertently torn a small hole in the hull. A small hole, but a hole none-the-less. During the past few hours, the entire bottom of the boat had been filling with water, and the bilge pumps were no match for this quantity of liquid influx. Ken quickly grabbed his cell phone and went to the top of the boat. He dialed 911. Fortunately, he was able to get an operator and explain the problem. The larger problem was that Ken had no idea where he was. He astutely narrowed it down to, "Somewhere on some river in the middle of the woods!" Night was falling fast, and the boat, still carrying over a hundred gallons of fuel, was going down in the middle of the environmental sensitive Ocala National Forest!

Before long a Sheriff's helicopter was circling the trees above them. They could not shoot a flare because, although they were about to get wet, the forest was very dry. Even Ken knew better than to add "forest fire" to their list of problems. Ken got back on the phone and described to the 911 operator each time he would hear the helicopter above them. Before long, the searchlights were on the boat. Almost an hour later, the first rescue boat arrived. By then, everything was completely submerged, except for the rooftop lounge area. Their "rescue boat" was actually a bass boat manned by a volunteer fireman, who lived down the river and heard the call on his scanner.

> Under the constitution of the United States, every man has the right to make a fool of himself as he sees fit.
>
> *Benjamin Franklin*

During the ordeal Ken called my house. Picking up the receiver I heard a static-y, "Were going down!" I thought he was kidding! Describing what had transpired, he went on to say that he and Steve were on the roof cooking steaks and lobster on the grill! Their reasoning was that, if they were going to die, they did not want to die hungry! He was not kidding! The following day the rescue-fireman said to me, "Yeah, when I got there, they were on the roof eating steaks and lobsters as fast as they could. The big one (referring to Ken) loaded about five cases of diet Mountain Dew onto my bass boat, as well as, a cooler full of food before we pulled away." That's my friend Ken. But the boat was about to be ancient history! To be honest with you, I don't miss that boat at all.

There is a great lesson here, which is this… It is often what you can't see that will kill you! My friends were moving along fine. They got comfortable meandering down the river, and quit watching the depth monitor. When they got into trouble, they tried to deal with it the simple way rather than diving in and cutting it off at the base. Yes, that would have been scary! I would have been scared to death to get in that water… under the boat… with the gators, but because they didn't do it—it cost them the entire vessel. Many people do this in life. They recognize their sinking condition; however, they choose to simply party the rest of their life away. Of course, they realize too late the consequences of their decision. If only they had "dived under the boat," they could have fixed the problem with a few pulls of the saw. If they were paying attention to the fact that they had a leak, they could have saved the vessel with a few inches of waterproof tape and let the bilge pumps do the rest of the work. It was a simple solution, but a solution ignored.

So… let's talk a minute. Let us try to find a parallel for our lives. First of all, keep your eyes peeled for the dangers below the water line. Beware of those secret sins that creep in to destroy. When, not if, you feel the impact of the evil one in your life, deal with the problem immediately. Cut it off at the root! Don't think you can eventually work yourself free and move on. You can't! It will rip at your hull until it eventually brings you down. Finally, make sure you fully repair the damages. Don't carry the baggage of past defeats. Let Christ rid you of that guilt before it seeps into your life, ultimately destroying the "vessel." One more thing…remove the captains hat, remember your position is that of deck hand.

Because we have grace should we continue in sin? No way! Nobody who has been freed from sin will want to walk in that sin any longer.
Romans 6:1-2

Baghdad This!

I don't understand the Muslim ladies who participate in the suicide bomb thing. Sure men get 72 virgins, but what do women get? Maybe they get 72 men clamoring for diner and the remote! That's something to die for? Duh!

Mike G. Williams

Okay, this is bothering me. I'm watching the Iraq War on CNN. The reporter has been interviewing some Iraqi citizens about their feelings toward the US. These same people have been gassed by their non-benevolent dictator. They have been beaten and imprisoned for harboring differing views from the BAATH Party. *Ironic that one would call it a "bath party" when these guys have lived in the desert for years without a bath.* This party, who is run at the whim of a tyrannical homicidal maniac named Saddam Hussein, has crippled the freedoms of his people for years. He has killed dissenters and deported others. Those were the lucky ones. As the Allied forces prepare to take Baghdad away from this political demon, however, the citizens complain about the country who is heading the charge. The country, which has given freedom to more nations than any other nation in the history of the world, is being berated by the soon-to-be free. The country striving to remove oppressors at the cost of many innocent lives, even coming with food, supplies, and money for those in need, is unappreciated by the very individuals it serves. These *bastions of ignorance* have the audacity to complain about the very hand that is freeing and feeding them. These ingrates have the audacity to attack the country

28

responsible for the Food for Oil program that allows their children to eat. I'm sorry if my bold statements offend you. It is just that I have seen this before and it makes no sense to me.

It wasn't long ago that my wife and I sponsored a young man's drug rehabilitation. This was a *Christian-based* program with a success rate among the highest in the country. The young man claimed a desire to be free from his addiction to *crack cocaine*, asking for the opportunity to go. After two days of being in the program, however, he wanted out. His reasons were similar to the Iraqi's. He wanted to "be free," but he wanted that freedom on his own terms. He didn't want an organization that touted Christianity to become his rescuer. That young man is now in a Texas prison…again. It makes no sense to me.

Many years ago my wife and I were called to a home to meet with two parents who were at their wits end. Their son was an addict. He finally reached a desperate point, pleading for help. The parents were absolutely thrilled! We met with them and began to discuss the options. The next day they went to see a particular rehabilitation program that we had suggested. They didn't contact us for a while. When the silence was eventually broken, they explained that, although they wanted their son to get off of drugs, they did not want him to become a "Jesus freak!" *I believe that was a direct quote.* They had toured the wonderful facility and were impressed by the number of success stories; however, they subsequently attended a chapel service. They said that the men had been turned into a bunch of shouting, praising, Jesus freaks. They did not want their son to become one of *those* people! They wanted him clean. They wanted him sober. But they didn't want him to become a *weirdo*. What a shame! *A deacon in the church did not want a kid who was crazy for Jesus.* They got what they wanted. Their son is not a Jesus freak… He died of an overdose last year. No, I did not do the funeral. I just couldn't.

> Those who differ with me have always caused me to learn more than those who have agreed with me.
>
> *Tim DeTellis*

Most of us want from God what we want, and we want what we want on our terms. "God bless my wishes, bless my desires, and complete that blessing in my way… Amen!" How arrogant can we get? How dare we look into the eyes of the potter and tell him how to fix our messes! I cannot believe people some times. It really makes me angry! But…let me confess for a minute. I do the same thing quite often. No, I am not a crack addict, but I have other issues. *Those of you who have seen me are thinking about the word " food" right now.* There are areas of my life that God is trying to correct and change and mend and rebuild, yet I keep fighting. I keep saying that I want the victory, but I want it on my own terms. I'm still looking for a conditional surrender. *I could handle a small plea bargain.* I don't want the help to come from that person, that place, or that other place. I want to be the master of my own future. O foolish man that I am! I want deliverance—but I don't want to go through detox!

> If lobsters looked like puppies, people could never drop them into boiling water while there still alive. I defy anyone to drop a living thing called "Buddy" in rapidly boiling water.
>
> *George Carlin*

Have you ever cried out for help and then criticized the help that came? Look deeper than the friends who helped with your latest house move. Look into the issues of your soul. Have you ever tried to bite the hand that was *spiritually* feeding you? Look into the areas of your life that are still being tortured by an evil dictator. What are you going to do about it? God is willing to radically change the person who is desperate enough to call out to Him without condition. *The words of Jesus always call us to a radical change.* His words often bite hard into our flesh! I can almost see the people walking away from Him as he said, "If you love this life you will lose it—but if you give up your life for me—you will keep it." I bet they wanted a compromise too. Righteous and complete healing rides on the train of obedience, never on the train of compromise. That is the plain and simple truth.

The person that trusts his or her own ability to change is a fool. The person who walks in Godly wisdom shall be delivered from troubles.
Proverbs 28:26

I Don't Have
the Legs for It

I think I might be addicted to second hand smoke which means I will have to go to a second hand store and find a used nicotine patch.

Tim Jones

*H*ave you ever listened to yourself sing? I like to fancy myself a singer, but then again so does almost everyone else in the known world. I know that we all sound relatively good in the shower, but what about in the closet… or better yet, on a recorder? That's definitely another story! *On tape I sound like a fourteen-year-old cat with a hairball caught in its larynx.* The invention of the Karaoke machine hasn't really helped the situation much either! I believe that people who say, "It isn't over until the fat lady sings," have never seen Karaoke. That particular "view" is usually just the beginning of a Karaoke evening. *Sorry! That is a cruel observation even if it does come from a guy one hundred pounds over his recommended weight!* But, let me continue to digress for a moment.

It must have been somewhere in the late seventies that soundtracks became available to the church crowd. These cassettes contained the instrumental music accompaniment to popular, contemporary religious songs. Unfortunately, for a few years this so-called "technological break-through" turned most Sunday morning services into a glorified karaoke bar with a tithing envelope replacing the two-drink minimum. I had quite a few of those tapes myself. At last count well over a hundred. So…I guess I am a bit of a hypocrite! Or maybe the quantity of soundtracks I own qualifies me to speak authoritatively on the subject. It's your decision. The tapes are now in a big Tupperware box in my garage, a monument to my youthful aspirations: Mike Williams—Recording Artist! *Has a nice ring to it, don't you think?* Unfortunately my vocal prowess did not match my vision of stardom! Sure, I made a living in music for many years, but I was no Garth Brooks. Heck, I wasn't even a Garth Swensen! *Garth Swensen was a student at a school I once attended. He didn't sing that well either.* Back in those school days I was trying to be the next Russ Taff or Sandi Patti. In retrospect, I don't know if I would have made a good Sandi. I don't have the legs for it!

The soundtracks of the seventies and eighties were a wonderful break from the accordion-accompanied songsters of the sixties and seventies. I remember one heavy-set lady who would get up every other Sunday and sing a song accompanied by her husband on the accordion. These people would climb the steps to the stage, and take their allotted three minutes just to get the one hundred pound accordion strapped on. Then the lady would launch into a bumbling three-minute dissertation on how she came to write this song at three in the morning after eating a large pepperoni pizza. The song always sounded like another song that she wrote and sang the week before last, only with slightly different words. She would always blurt out, "Pray for me as I sing this song." *As a teenager I would mumble, "Hey, how about praying for us, lady, we gotta hear it? Pray the accordion breaks; pray for juvenile, immediate onset deafness; pray for the rapture!"* My parents would remind me that it wasn't what a person sounded like; it was the heart behind it. Well these folks must have had some really big hearts! Unfortunately, those hearts were being hidden behind a really big annoying accordion! I can't be sure, but if you ask me, they were allowed to sing because they were business owners and thus big donors! *This wasn't singing, it was sacrificial mourning in irregular polka rhythm.*

It's been twenty-five years now and I have softened a bit. I may finally understand what my parents meant by the whole *"heart"* thing. Not that I have come to believe that anyone with a big heart should be allowed to publicly *bellow* like a water buffalo, but time has given me a greater ability to recognize the "heart" now.

> Everyone wants to be delivered—nobody wants to go through detox!
> *Mike G. Williams*

A few weeks ago I was in Vancouver (that's in Canada for you non-geography buffs) for the Christian Camping Association Conference. This *most excellent* event included seminars, exhibits, great food, worship, special music, a little humor from me, and Dr. Joe Stowell as the guest speaker. I arrived early just in time to get in on Dr. Stowell and his biblical insights. *He is always inspirational, introspective, and informative.* I listen to him on the radio all the time. It was a great conference, and I went away well rewarded for my services. The greatest reward I received came not through a seminar, speaker, or paycheck, however. The "reward moment" for me happened during a song time.

> Don't you ever get discouraged when you wake up and realize you have to wash again?
>
> *George Carlin*

Our worship leader was a mesmerizing young African-American. He had all the "stuff" musically. His voice was like an angel, an angel with a three-octave range. His keyboard prowess was absolutely flawless and very tasteful, and his band could easily have accompanied anyone on the circuit. I don't need to say all this, but I want you to understand fully the comparison I am going to make. The "reward moment" that I mentioned in the last paragraph came in a different way than expected. The emcee explained that our music that night would include a special guest. As he began to share about this guest, one could see an older gentleman feebly approaching the stage. He explained that our guest was a friend of Christian camping, a godly Christian gentleman, a decorated war veteran, and former Prisoner of War who saw action in numerous places including the D-Day invasion. As the old man reached the center of the stage and placed his wrinkled hands squarely on either side of the podium, the audience could see that he did this for much- needed balance. His countenance definitely revealed a number of years had been lived in this frail frame. The music began to play behind him, "La, la, la, la, la-la, la, la, la, la, la…." As the old man began to sing "Great is Thy faithfulness… O God my Father," his voice cracked as he continued, "There is no shadow of turning with Thee… Thou changest not, Thy compassions they fail not… As thou has been, Thou forever will be…" You could feel the emotion sweep the room as grown men began to weep. I was one of those. I can't help but shed a tear, even today, as I relive that moment. There was a man who truly knew the faithfulness of God. There was a man who had walked through the "Valley of the Shadow of Death" and felt the "Unseen Hand" on his shoulder. He finished the verse, and we all took a breath, probably the first one since he began. Then with all the vocal intensity that a great gospel singer can deliver, the young worship leader raised his voice to belt out the second verse. That was good…and he was good. We needed a break from the emotion of the moment, if for nothing more than gathering composure. After giving the old man a little time to catch his breath during that verse, the worship leader played a short musical interlude and this elderly gentleman launched into his final verse. "Pardon for sin, and a peace that endureth… Thine own dear presence, to cheer and to guide… Strength for each day, and hope for tomorrow… Blessings all mine, and ten thousand beside…" The audience of men and women, youth workers and seniors alike without encouragement began to join the elderly gentleman in that powerful chorus. We sang with voices cracking under the strain of the lumps in our throats. You see, this was not a man singing words printed on a page, this was a "heart" singing…a heart that had lived through hell and yet, had experienced the faithfulness of God. This was the heart of Job who said, "Though he slay me yet will I trust Him!" This was the heart of Abraham who raised the knife above Isaac only to see a ram caught in the thicket! This was the heart of the three Hebrews who walked through the fire with the Son of God! This was the heart of Stephen who lifted up his eyes toward heaven as the flying stones would usher him to his God! We sang loudly, we sang softly, we choked back the tears as *inspired* words flowed from our trembling lips. "Great is Thy faithfulness, Great is Thy faithfulness… Morning by morning new mercies I see… All I have needed Thy hands have provided… Great is Thy faithfulness, Lord unto me."

I guess now I understand what my parents meant when they talked about the heart. It is the "heart" behind a song that truly makes the song worth hearing. May my heart be able to live that which I sing, and may you also be fortunate enough to truly experience the faithfulness of the God of which you sing before you meet Him. Need I say more? I think not.

Be fully aware that the Lord your God is a faithful God, He keeps covenants and shows mercy to those who love Him, and keep His commandments for a thousand of generations.
Deuteronomy 7:9

Returnable Bottles

Last Christmas I ran out of Christmas wrapping paper and had to use Happy Birthday paper. So I creatively took out a marker and wrote JESUS at the end of every phrase. Everyone thought it was a good Idea, well everyone but my Jewish friends

Mike G. Williams

*I*t was in my sophomore year of high school. It was a cruel trick, but it seemed was funny at the time. You see, my parents had placed their child (me) in a Christian school because the public schools were having a slight problem with me. *Is that a nice way of saying that I got expelled a few (seven) times?* Nevertheless, I found a few ways to torture my new captures.

I have mentioned and described the principal of one particular school in past stories, so I will not wax eloquent in that area today. I will just say that, from time to time, my good friend Don and I reciprocated creatively for the stern discipline he brought to our lives.

On the days we would skip school, one of our favorite things to do was take a drive in the country. For us, the country was that area south of town where the orange groves go on for miles and the phosphate pits are burgeoning with

> I must surrender my fascination with myself to a more worthy preoccupation with the character and purposes of God. I am not the point. He is. I exist for Him. He does not exist for me.
>
> *Larry Crabb*

largemouth bass. It was a great place for a school-skipping kid to fish and hunt for snakes. We loved to hunt snakes. It was practically a God-given calling on our lives. Ironically, our dear principal had his home a few miles from our favorite lunker holes, so the occasion to go roaring past his house every time we took an unauthorized break from school was unfortunately inevitable.

Sometimes idle hands can be the Devil's workshop. *Sometimes hands that are busily working on a fishing reel or holding a bag containing a snake can be rather "Devil's workshop-ee" too.* Knowing that our principal's wife, who was a teacher at the school, was gone from their home as well, was enough to get our brains catapulted into thinking up some mischief. Now believe me, we never broke into the home and vandalized it. We never caused any major property damage, well, at least not to my recollection.

> Negotiation instructors have told me to never ask a question you don't already know the answer to. How did these people graduate from Kindergarten?
>
> *Jim Hinder*

The pranks we pulled were designed to inflict emotional distress. *We liked to think of it as karma although I doubt God will see it that way on Judgment Day.* Outside of the occasional dead water moccasin that we would put in his mailbox, our evil devises were meant to cause embarrassment similar to the way he liked to embarrass us in front of our peers. He was a young principal, working for minuscule pay and learning his leadership style by trial and error. We simply became the opportune guinea pigs for his first appointment to the bench. On days that we skipped school, we became the jury for his trial and errors.

Our vigilantes often reared its ugly head in rather interesting forms. There were a few times when we ordered magazine subscriptions for him. We would go to the drug store magazine rack and remove the subscription cards for twenty different magazines, sending them all in for him checked, "Bill me later!" Of course, there were the times we put Democratic campaign signs in his front yard. *For a Conservative Independent Baptist, this was tantamount to having beer in the refrigerator!* And...yes...we did that also. Well, not exactly in the refrigerator, but close to it. One of my neighbors was a beer drinker, and a beer-can recycler! So, every single can he drank, which numbered to about a case worth a night, went into large plastic bags next to the door of his lovely singlewide. During the day, when he was gone to work *at the nuclear power plant*, the beer cans were simply there for the picking. Therefore, on occasion, the good principal would come home to find empty Bud cans all over their back porch. Sometimes we would scatter them around the front door, and occasionally we would come by at night and place a few in the back of his pickup truck. There are a few pranks that I will not tell you about. That was a long time ago, and I have since repented.

In Michigan they have a ten-cent deposit on plastic bottles. They have a deposit on cans too. New York only has a five-cent deposit. I didn't know that until last week. I guess I have seen that "return for deposit" printed on cans before, but never really paid much attention to it. It's not like I'm going to fill my Jeep with cans and make a quick trip from Florida to Michigan for the spare change. Certainly not to New York for a mere five cents! *Those cheap Yankees!*

In my household we recycle! Every aluminum can, two liter cola bottle, grocery bag, used batteries, *unused nuclear waste*, magazines, or plastic containers of any type are deposited into the yellow box for the Monday pick-up. Yes, I have reasons! First of all it saves our country millions of dollars in oil usage. *So, in a way, it is how I am personally fighting the Taliban!* Recycling also cuts down on the pollutants in our landfills, and probably most importantly, because they gave me a free yellow box! *Oh, also because I have read the book of Genesis. You know, where Phil Collins reminds us to recycle.* See, I take God's command to manage the earth as seriously as I can without sacrificing my SUV on a biodegradable recycled stone altar. Certainly I don't believe that SUV owners are going to spend eternity in Hades, but maybe their vehicle rollover statistics are God's way of telling them something. *I have no idea what.*

> The great sin of the world is not that the human race has failed to work for God so as to increase His glory, but that we have failed to delight in God so as to reflect His glory. For Gods' glory is most reflected in us when we are most delighted in Him.
>
> *John Piper*

When I was a young kid in Illinois we had the returnable glass bottles, but not any more. It's a disposable world, and the "choice of a new generation" is not just Pepsi—it's plastic! I still miss the taste of a Coke from a sixteen-ounce glass bottle. Glass tastes better! Do you have any idea what I'm talking about? They still have and use the glass bottles in the country of Haiti. It's one of the little perks of visiting a country that is still mainly without electricity. I guess I was eight or ten when I discovered I could collect discarded bottles from the roadside and hide them in my closet. Sometimes my friends and I would steal them from a neighbor's porch. *I will have to confess that tonight in my evening prayers* When I finally collected enough bottles to equal a dollar or two, I would cart them to the grocery store. It was kind of like an allowance for a poor kid! One time I saved up enough to buy a model airplane; usually, it was just candy or gum.

There were times when my mom would come into my room and ask for the bottles. *I knew why.* Two empty eight-packs could buy a few cans of tomato soup or a family size Beef-a-roni for supper. When you're in a family, you have to give and help where you can. Sometimes Mom would have me go out looking for bottles to buy dinner. You can look pretty diligently when your supper depends on finding the glass treasures.

When I look back on my life, I see the diligence I gave to so many things. There were stupid things and silly things. I also see my persistent ability to work for family meals during those tough times. I wonder if I would work that hard for my spiritual food… as if I had to do that. I wonder if I would go out and search for bottles or collect cans if my spiritual well-being depended on it. *Heck, I often struggle to find the effort to get off the couch to retrieve a Max Lucado book from the shelf, much less a Bible.* I want to be a person who strives hard after the spiritual nourishment of God. It is a daily struggle. It is too easy to become complacent and satisfied with the junk food that I find lying around the house, on the television, and on the radio. Not that there isn't some phenomenal Christian programming available, but I usually even bypass that for an *All in the Family* re-run.

Can I challenge you, as I challenge myself, to develop and cultivate a *need* for the Word of God? Force-feed yourself the genuine Good News until your mind and body develops a hunger and craving for it. Keep reaching for the quality Bread of Life, and don't settle for the day-old bakery brand. Drink daily from the milk of the Word and don't settle for yesterday's fill. And remember…don't leave your returnable bottles on your back porch. I may need some soup money someday and drive to Michigan!

Desire the Word of God as babies desire the milk. This is where your growth comes from.
1 Peter 2:2

A.D.D.

I was filling out a questionnaire in the doctors office, and the question said, Do you have conversations with people who are not really there? I wrote, how would I know?

Mike G. Williams

I have ADD. *I don't mean that in a mathematical way.* It is more commonly called Attention Deficit Disorder. If you are not familiar with it, you have been living on an island for the past ten years. Okay Skipper, let me explain further. ADD is a basically a problem that manifests itself in one's inability to focus. I've had it since I was a kid, but when I was a kid, it was not something for which you received medication. *It was something for which you got spanked.* It should have been called ABNB, as more appropriately referred to as A Butt Needs Beat!

I'm forty years old, which means, I grew up a few years before the invention of *Ritalin®*. I was ripped off! Cheated! It wasn't fair! I grew up under an experimental medication called the *belt*. I'm sure a few of you grew up under that medication as well. It was quite effective in bringing me back into focus, albeit, rather abruptly. In fact, in my childhood, had the belt have been a registered medication I would have had a leather IV on full drip. I got the belt rather often.

In the 60's there was no ADD or ADHD. By the way, the letter *H* adds the word *hyperactivity* to the mix of meaning. It means that not only does a person have the inability to focus, they also enjoy running around the room at the speed of a *hamster on crack* as they continue to not-focus. As

I think back, I should have had that version of it. *At least then I would have been harder to catch, thus harder to spank.* Maybe my father would have gotten so worn out catching me that his medicating arm would have been weak. My dad, however, must have been ambidextrous. To be real honest, I can't help but feel that many ADD and ADHD cases I see today could be completely solved with a stout piece of mahogany or perhaps a flat piece of leather. Medication should never be used in place of good discipline, although there are cases where medication is needed. *I think I should have been one of those kids!*

I think I might have had ADLBD. The acrostic is my own creation, but I have met other people who swear their kids have it. ADLBD is my acrostic for *Attention Deficit Lazy-Butt Disorder.* My mind wandered although my body preferred to lie on the couch. The fact is, most people do not understand ADD or ADHD. They believe that a child (or adult) suffering from this malady cannot, or chooses not to focus. The truth is, we can focus, but not necessarily on just one thing. *That* is the problem. We focus on everything. Take me for a ride in the car and I can tell you every business we passed on our route. I can tell you what was down every side street. I can tell you about weird posters I saw in the windows of stores as we careened past. I can tell you in great detail about a unique car I saw during the journey and someone of interest along the way. I can point out unique absurdities in signage." But, if you feel I am not focusing on what you said, you may be half right. Oh, I heard you, but I may have not processed what you said at the time you said it. *It may be next week.* I will have to get back to you on that. It is a little hard for me to focus right now.

> People who dance are considered insane by those who can't hear the music.
>
> *George Carlin*

As I got older I graduated from the belt to the board, a three-foot long, six-inch wide piece of cedar that was often applied to my bare bottom. My dad drilled about fourteen holes in the board. *He believed it would make the board more aerodynamically balanced.* And it did! As a side effect, however, I ended up with little red circles all over my cheeks, closely resembling little hickeys. *Now, hickeys on one's butt are really hard to explain in a gym class.* My friends had quite a few laughs telling each other that my dad gave me hickeys on my butt. I know it's not funny to those of us who have reached a state of maturity, but to a seventh-grade boy it was a *hootable* line.

Interesting thing this ADD. It never goes away. Maturity helps fight it, but not cure it. I have been prayed over! Yes, after talking about this at a few churches, the elders gathered around me and prayed. Some rather vigorously, I must say. During which time I would meticulously concentrate on their prayer...*And* I would concentrate on the guy in front of me with bad breath...*And* I would concentrate on the guy whose tie only came down to his navel, yet the tail extended much farther... I also wondered if a circle of prayer for his fashion sense would be helpful, as I concentrated on the fact that there were twelve chairs in the room and that one of them appeared to be broken and another one was missing a rubber floor bumper. I wondered how that would really affect the carpet over the long run. *Then* I considered what types of carpet would best detour this problem. *Then* I thought about a detour sign I had seen in

> How many ADD kids does it take to change a light bulb? Hey—what time is it?
>
> *Mike G. Williams*

Shreveport Louisiana when I was there for a concert. Then I thought about the time I called the airport authority in that town and told them their airport was shabbier than the airport in Port O Prince, Haiti. *In addition* I thought about the conversation I had which included the information that Shreveport had become a unionized baggage-handling airport, and the service had gone down since that time. *That made me think* about legendary union boss, Jimmy Hoffa and wondered if we would ever find his body...*And* I thought about a funny song I sing about Jimmy Hoffa that nobody in the younger generation understands, and how that is a real shame because it is a very funny song. *Then* I thought about Hoffa's connection to John F. Kennedy and wondered if there really was a conspiracy and the implications today if President Johnson really had been involved. That was when I began to recollect about the old thirty-five horse-powered Johnson motor that I had on a boat once. I think that that engine was probably the finest built engine to ever grace the boating industry. I remember one time when I was on Lake Chetec in Wisconsin that the carburetor had worked itself loose from the housing. The bolts had fallen out, and I had to drive the boat to the marina with my hand up in the cowling, holding the carburetor body in place. They were relatively simple carburetors compared to the Quadrajet carburetors that my dad taught me to overhaul when I was a kid. I learned to do them after Dad would get mad and throw them across the room and storm out. He would shout, "I'll never be able to go to work now and I don't care anymore!" I would go over and patiently assemble it and bring it to him. Those were a few of the times when I was the "good son" who knew about carburetors, which would prove helpful seeing that I was "never going to amount to anything if I did not get my grades up." Hey, I think I just heard an "amen." Did you know that the word *amen* means *so be it.* If that is true, people need to be careful where they shout it. I feel better now. "Oh… there done praying." I think that prayer really helped me. I think. Maybe I will have more time to think about that later. When the group had stopped praying for me I was free to offer a humble "thanks" and go my way. The next day I would try to think about their prayers for me and about all the other stuff too.

The apostle Paul says, "This one thing I do…" *One thing!* Could there be anything harder for me? Paul could have said, "I like to levitate and so should everyone else." Levitation would probably be easier for me! Paul, however, declares that he focuses singular attention on the mark, the prize of the high calling of Jesus Christ. He chooses to forget those things that are behind him and press forward toward his calling in Christ Jesus. He often refers to forcing his mind and body into submission. He kind of spanks himself! I guess they didn't have medication back then. Maybe ADD was Paul's "thorn in the flesh."

The Psalmist writes of the dangers of being "double-minded." *Dang! I struggle with triple minded, quadruple minded, or septuplet minded! Is septuplet* a number word? I was thinking about the McCaughey septuplets and how I think the word represents a count of seven. My agent also represents the McCaughey's. Since when did you need an agent when you had seven kids? My grandfather had twenty kids, and he didn't have an agent; he didn't even have a car. That was many years ago and times have changed. *Oh, there I go again, let me get back to the point, sorry.*

> Wherever you are, be all there. Live life to the hilt every situation you believe to be the will of God.
>
> *Jim Elliot*

I so very much want to be truly focused on my walk with God. I truly want to be focused on my relationship with Christ. I truly want to be led by the Spirit each and every minute, but it is a struggle. The "bringing of the mind into captivity" is a constant struggle. Maybe you have been thinking that you are alone in your struggle. You are not. I am struggling along with you. I'm struggling with all of my might to stay focused on the right stuff and to not be distracted by the things of this world. I'm struggling to stay focused on the journey. I look forward to the day I will receive my new body and my new mind. That will be a great day! Let's talk that day, shall we? Maybe we can truly listen to each other then. *Wow! Check it out! There's a piece of fossilized gum shaped like Jimmy Hoffa's head stuck to the bottom of my chair! I can feel it! It's like facial Braille! I wish I could learn Braille!*

I so want to be single minded. Pray for me! I will pray for you! And strive with all of your might to focus in on the important things in life. You know what they are.

Press toward the mark for the prize of the high calling of God in Christ Jesus. And as we desire to live rightly, God shall reveal to us our double-mindedness that we may be changed.
Philippians 3:14-15

Stop the Music You Pitch Impaired Pinhead

My Mudder use't tw-oo let me lwick the beaters on hwer cake mixer, one twime they was still spa-winning. Dwat hwurt!

Mike G. Williams

*T*hose aging country vocal chords rang out, *"And Lord for my sake, please help me to take, one day at a time."* I have always hated that song! Can I detest this song to a greater degree? No! The writer of this song should be flogged and then taken to a river and made to drink downstream from the cattle. This is one of the most pathetic examples of Christian narcissism that I have ever seen. *You know me, I don't mean to be negative in any way.* OK…OK…Yes, I do! Have you heard this song? Better yet, have you heard the golden vocals of Christy Lane singing it on her "buy my worthless out-of-date music" infomercial? She still has it available on 8-track. It is good to know that Christy is keeping up with current trends in the audio circles. "Hey Christy, they got a new thing now called CD's that are really catching on! Sell that 1980 Ford Pinto and join the rest of us here in century twenty-one."

Another problem is this song entitled *Why Me Lord?* This is a simple question that has been asked throughout the centuries by such greats as Job, Noah, David, and Kris Kristofferson. I think I heard that Kris wrote this song while in rehab from taking far too much heroin. I could be wrong. The line in the song for which I have the greatest disdain is found in the second verse. Those immortal words, "Lord you know, if you are looking below, it's worse now than then, there is pushing and shoving, and crowding my mind…" Yep! Our difficulties are so much worse today than two thousand years ago. We have car problems… You, Lord, didn't have them! We have poor fast-food service problems… You didn't have them! We have lousy hotel concierge service… You didn't have that in Bethlehem, I'll bet! We have dirty convenient stores… You didn't have those! We have "pushing, shoving, and crowding my microscopic mind…" All He had was that crucifixion thing! Yep! We have it pretty bad! Lord if you're looking below, I'm certain You can see how much worse it is. Bull!

> The deepest pleasures in life don't satisfy—they point us forward. Until we attain unity with Christ in heaven, an inconsolable longing for more will remain in every human heart.
>
> *Larry Crabb*

People, we've got it good! Very good! When I consider all that those before me experienced, I am very grateful to have been born in this generation. Although each generation offers its share of troubles, we have been very blessed with conveniences like never before. Have you stopped to consider lately how good you have it? I sure hope you have. I hope that you are daily thanking God for the blessings of the day. I believe that one of the things that grieves God the most, is an ungrateful heart, and *that kind* of heart runs rampant today. I have to fight it. The media proclaims the phrase "You Deserve More!" And if we are not careful we will buy into it. I often do.

The "You Deserve More" is a popular slogan these days. Whether that be for people who have ruined their credit from purchasing worthless trinkets on the Home Shopping Network or people who have lied and cheated their way into bankruptcy. Where, in the pursuit of happiness, is the "You Deserve More" concept given? Where in the Bible is the "You Deserve More" concept given? Certainly the Gospel offers grace to those who have chosen to run from God and mess up their lives. *But, that is grace.* Grace is given because we deserve to be punished for our sins and can't handle the punishment. Grace is given because we *do not* deserve another chance. Grace is given because we have extended our moral credit beyond the limit and could *never* pay it back.

The problem with the "You Deserve More" mentality is that it breeds ingratitude. It says that all men are basically good, and if something bad happened, it is certainly not my fault. It is someone else's fault; thus, "You Deserve" another five or six (or sixty) chances. The truth is that Mike

Williams does not deserve more chances. Mike Williams has been a thief and a liar! Mike Williams has been an extorter and a coveter. Mike Williams has willfully broken almost every law in the book, at least in his mind. Mike Williams has overcharged people for second-rate work. Mike Williams has made promises he had no intention of keeping. Mike Williams has led people to believe things that were not true. *Mike Williams once stole a plaque of the Ten Commandments!* Mike Williams does not deserve more! Mike deserves HELL! If my moment of honesty is a bit much for you, get over it. I know me better that you know me—so shut up.

> If you want to feel rich, just count all the things you have that money can't buy.
>
> *Daniel Webster*

I love the song that says, "It's only by grace we can enter…and only by grace we can stand…" I sit here in this hotel room remembering that I have been given way more than I deserve. The last breath I draw into these tired old lungs will be a gift from God. The fact that you would give your hard-earned money to purchase these ramblings of mine is much more than I deserve. If you all sent the books back and demanded a refund, you would not be without that right. *Not that I would refund you anything, so don't get any ideas.* The fact that I have been allowed to be a husband to a wonderful wife is more than I deserve. The fact that I have been allowed to influence and experience the love of my children is more than I deserve. It is also a privilege that they will have to pay a price for in the future. *Can you say counseling?*

So… Mike has been very blessed! Very graced! Very over-loved! I fall on my face and say "Thank You God!" Thank you for undeserved grace. You have been blessed as well, my friend. We are not so different. Am I right? Dang straight!

By grace we are saved through faith.
We had nothing to do with this God gift…
so don't be too haughty about it.
Ephesians 2:8

I Couldn't Break Out of a Plastic Bag

Life is short, travel light, or get a large van to hold all your stuff.
Mike G. Williams

J love watching Biography. It would be dangerous if I had cable television at home, I would probably never leave the set. In fact, when I'm at a hotel most of my writing is done with Biography or the History Channel playing in the background. I have to admit that I am also very partial to watching VH-1's Where Are They Now. *It helps me to know that all of my childhood heroes are now in rehab or at least have their names on the walk of fame at the Betty Ford Clinic.* It makes me feel better about my life. *I'm not picking on Betty, the truth is that I wouldn't recognize Betty Ford if she staggered up to me at a party.* Cruel or not, that was an insightful historical reference.

Last night I typed this book's introduction while watching a semi-documentary about the great escape from the Mecklenburg Prison. Six death row inmates, seeing their end insight, masterminded a scheme to escape from an inescapable maximum-security prison. They did it through a series of false rumors and impersonations and soon found themselves on the outside. Six death row inmates who had been convicted of killing over seventeen people and thought to have killed many more, were now running the roads in police issue riot gear. It was amazingly interesting to me how they pulled it off. Let me try and describe it. Please understand that I am going to tell you a two-hour story in a few sentences. *This is a man thing.* My wife would include the attire of the inmates and the style of their hair. I, on the other hand, will give you the basic facts and my keen observation as a trained professional T.V. watcher, a virtual master of spotting (even while watching a crime-scene re-creation) the most inconceivably miniscule bits of evidence the police might overlook.

The inmates spread rumors that the men in cell block C were building a bomb. Guards searched and found nothing. While playing basketball in the yard, one inmate faked a knee injury. *It is obvious to me (in the recreation) the inmate was faking it because he did not limp in a very realistic manner. The guards should have seen that.* This left a smaller number of guards than necessary to supervise this gang of killers. *Familiarity always breeds contempt!* The inmates began to scuffle in the hall allowing one of the inmates to sneak into a private bathroom to hide. When the central door supervisor moved from his desk for a moment, he propped open his office door. This allowed the hidden inmate to unlock all the doors. From that point it was simply a majority of inmates overpowering the guards and putting on their uniforms. The guards found themselves without their clothes, tied in a closet. A frantic call to the main gate, informing them to open both gates for a prison van disposing of a bomb, was met with immediate obedience.

> Familiarity breeds contempt... whereas rabbits always breed rabbits... how weird is that?
> *Gordon Douglas*

It was poetry in motion orchestrated by a guy who had not gone beyond the sixth grade. In retrospect they discovered that the flaws in the security system were basically a series of little mistakes made by the guards. *You could say that the guards "let their guard down."* Their familiarity with these evil men gave them a false sense of security. They began to, almost, befriend these murderers. They allowed little fluctuations in the rules such as allowing themselves to be outnumbered during transportations and the simple act of propping open a door because it was easier than asking for assistance. The inmates used fear (the bomb rumor) to allow another guard to blindly follow instructions and open the outermost main gate. Now, if you saw the program or were around in 1984 for the actual event, you know the inmates were soon caught. When the inmates separated from their "brain" man, they quickly fell back into their ignorant ways. *Talk about some tense moments in between commercial breaks!*

What great lessons for my life! There is this evil man, a condemned man, living inside of me, trying to get out and get in, and trying to wage war against the guardian of my soul. He is getting more threatening as he sees his end is near. I must be careful *not* to become *too* comfortable with his friendly smile attempting to mask his evil ways. I must not become too familiar with him. I should not trust him. I should not let my guard down. I should be aware that he watches for my repeated mistakes and will use them against me to ensnare me and leave me naked in the closet. My enemy wants me to leave the door propped open for his evil cohorts, Pride and Rebellion, to take control of all the doors of my mind. Is it any wonder that my good buddy Paul,

> Those who think they have arrived, have lost their way. Those who think they have reached their goal, have missed it. Those who think they are saints, are demons.
>
> *Henri Nouwen*

who knew a little about prisons himself, used to say that there was a war going on inside his flesh? He proclaimed that he often did the things he knew he shouldn't do; and the things he knew he should do, he often neglected. He said if it were not for the ultimate victory that comes through the Chief Warden, we would be hopeless. I certainly would be.

So today, consider the areas of your heart where you have let loose what should be held captive. Where have you let your guard down? Where has familiarity allowed you to put yourself in places where you were outnumbered? Where have you propped the doors open? Where have you let the captive sneak into your bathroom? I think you know what I mean. Was your mind left open today? Ears?

Through God's strength we can recognize and protect the areas of our minds that harbor evil thoughts and unrighteous desires. In His strength we can bring our thought life under the control of Christ.

2 Corinthians 10:5

They Have Seen
Other Hats

*I believe in... support... and even celebrate diversity.... I just wish
we could all dress neatly and sit quietly while we are celebrating it.*

Mike G. Williams

I think it's funny! I found myself staring at this policeman in the
Pittsburgh International Airport. Have you seen the police hats
with the chinstrap, the chinstrap that comes down to right below their
mouths? It runs from ear to ear, and hangs in front of their face, just
below their lower lip. It resembles a horse's bridal gone bad, or possibly
a tiny leather brassier for a sagging lower lip. I have seen them in
Pennsylvania and Ohio. I'm sure there are also a few other places that
said, "Hey that looks oddly dignified, let's try it." Now, there are probably some good reasons that the hat straps are designed like this. Maybe
it is in memorial to the first state patrolman whose hat strap did not fit
properly. Maybe it is to remind the men
that they are to be listening rather than
talking. I mean, seriously, the strap
clearly impedes conversation. *Maybe it
is to improve the appearance of the
mouth-breathers.* You know the guys,
the ones who wander around with their mouth opened, jawbones fully
extended, seemingly unable to breathe through their nostrils. *They are
often named Bubba or Scooter and physically resemble their aunt-momma,
but with less facial hair.* But why the need for the strap? Was there was a

> First of all—Shut Up!
>
> *Randy Horton*

severe leather shortage at the police hat factory? Is this weird strap some type of aid to their image? *Is there some profiler out there who determined that people with an ill-fitting chinstrap look more authoritative than those with a properly fitting one?* This same logic says that people with food hanging from their chin or, possibly, a booger hanging from their nose are more physically attractive. C'mon, this has got to seriously limit clear communication. I can hear potential defendants at trial claiming that they did not know what the officer was saying. "I couldn't hear what the officer was saying. His lip kept getting snarled up in the (ever-so-stylish) lower-lip strap. He could have been saying, "Stop! Police! But it sounded as if he was ordering a kielbasa in native Polish." Which I have done!

> If at first you don't succeed—gather all the evidence and burn it so no one knows you tried.
> **Dan Nolt**

Do these guys know how silly it looks? I'm sure they do. They have been to the law enforcement conventions; they know the options. They understand that straps can be made longer. There is no leather or shiny plastic shortage that I know of. *Neither is their any prize for looking ludicrous.* They could claim they didn't realize what they looked like, but it's just like having your zipper down, somebody will eventually tell you. Seeing that I often have the occasion to personally meet these men of legal authority while traveling down the Interstate, however, I had better move along in my description and include some proper respect. I should also include the fact that these fine men and women do not have any choice in their wardrobe. It is standard uniform issue!

Let me digress a moment. I think the short chinstrap is best used to help keep mouths shut, which is an admirable trait in anybody. There it is, a constant little leather reminder that they need to listen first. Can good judgments be made through talking? *I think not* What good information can be gleaned in the process of sharing what one

> I walked a mile with chatter... and she rambled all the way... leaving me none the wiser than I was yesterday. I walked a mile with silence... never a word said she... but all the things I learned the day that silence walked with me.
> **Mike G. Williams**
> (adapted from an old poem)

already knows? Very little! I think we all could use a lower lip strap! I know I could.

The Bible states that we are to be people who are lip restrained. Slow to speak! We are also people who need to show some restraint in our actions. Quick judgments often bring about mistakes and misgivings. Quick judgments and quick wit, if you want to call it that, have moved me to many apologies. What about you? What have you learned from your forays into blabbing? Have you learned to slow the pace your mind to lip-connections? I hope so.

Let us be people who are listeners first, then slow to speak, and then very slow to act in judgment.
James 1:19

Take Me Out to the Ball Game

My life used to be nothing but drinking, fighting, and foul language until I decided to quit church softball.

Tim Hawkins

I remember the first time my coach asked me to bunt. No way! Bunting is for sissies. I wanted to knock it over the fence! The girls date the "over-the-fence" guys, not the "bunt" guys. "Bunt" is for cakes; home runs are for real men, like me, of course. But, the coach wanted me to bunt in an attempt to bring Bob Ward into home plate. Bob was big, but fast. He just needed a break to score. Well I bunted, Bob came home, and the girls gathered around Bob for winning the game. *Are they idiots?* I won the game with my *sissy-boy* bunt. The school paper lauded the glorious win and cited Bob as the school hero. One day the High School Hall of Fame will set the record straight, I'm sure. I will be vindicated! *And so will Pete Rose!*

A baseball historian is trying to change major league baseball's RBI (runs batted in) record. He desires to do this before Juan Gonzalez of the Texas Rangers can break it. Clifford Kachline, formerly with the National Baseball Hall of Fame, says the RBI record currently on the books is 190 but should be 191. Hack Wilson of the Chicago Cubs set the record in 1930. He claims it was an official scorekeeper's mistake. Kachline has claimed that the scorekeeper shortchanged the Cubs slugger during a game against Cincinnati on July 28, 1930. Maybe the guy was sleeping or out for a potty break. Researchers say that newspaper accounts verify the missing mysterious RBI. Kachline and other historians say they researched all of Wilson's other RBI's that year the same way, and came up with 191. He will present the information to official record keepers. *Now that they have this behind them, they can get around to my trophy!*

I imagine that most of my readers are saying, "Who cares? That was sixty-plus years ago! Well sixty-plus for the Cub's guy anyway, and we are talking about RBI's, so who cares? Homeruns are one thing, but RBI's?" Well, in my book, RBI's are the main thing. You see, I believe in team players. Give me an employee who wants to see a co-worker have success, and I will show you a great employee and a winning individual. Show me a church that honestly prays for the success of the church down the road, even the one whose people *raise their hands,* or the one *who does not raise their hands,* or the one who has a statue of St. Peter in their front yard, and I will show you a church that I want to attend. This is a Church that realizes the vastness of the body of Christ. This is a church that realizes that God is bigger than they are.

Billy Graham's teammates have to be some of the leading RBI players in the Christian league. Night after night these men and women have gotten onto the field and helped drive others toward home. They are the bus drivers, the prayer warriors, the pamphlet passers, the ushers, and the behind the scenes support staff, who allow people to get knocked into home. It is not bothersome to them if the media looks at Billy as the most eloquent player in the league. Their concern is only that Billy gets up to bat.

> If I could be anything... I would like to be hotdog... with mustard all over me... then if I got hungry I could just eat myself... oh yeah... oh yeah!
>
> *Will Ferrell*
> (playing the part of Harry Carey on SNL)

I hope you can see the parallel for you and me. Certainly, I want to stand at the plate as often as possible and swing with all of my might so that I might move people along in their faith walk. I say "people," but I will include my friends, family, even my children. It is easy for a person in the spotlight (we are all in that spotlight from time to time) to work only for the big home run. The big show! The big moment! When the truth is that we have often been called to bunt. That's right! We are asked to bunt or even make a sacrifice fly. That might be working in the nursery, rather than singing in the choir. That might be cleaning the water closets rather than serving communion. We are asked to lay down personal stardom for the sake of the kingdom.

> There are many of us that are willing to do great things for the lord, but few are willing to do little things.
>
> *D. L. Moody*

I may never get the most RBI's in this game either. That's okay. It is simply important that I am supporting the team with every opportunity I have. It is important that I am willing to "take one for the team" if needed; and, one day, I will get to ultimately come home myself. PTL! Are you willing to be a team player? Or will you only participate if you can be a star? Think about it!

We are called to live together in one accord, walking in love, admiring the gifts of others, and humbly considering each other above ourselves.
Philippians 2:2-3

Life Happens—
Deal With It

Countries are making nuclear weapons like there's no tomorrow.

Emo Philips

Don't ask for all the details, but I was wearing a giant bear suit. Now, I have done some stupid things over the years, but this one ranks up at the top. Let me explain. Being the only one on the Dominican Crusade Team who could not speak Spanish, I was given the bear-suit job. No language skills needed, but the ability to grunt and hold a sign directing children to the tent was a must. The grunt is apparently a universal sound. Obviously the bears in Spanish-speaking countries do not grunt with a Spanish accent. So… here I am, over six feet tall and weighing in at—well, let's just say, a few pounds over the legal ladder-climbing limit—in a bear suit with no ventilation. It is 105 degrees in the shade. My sweat is pouring an acid rain concoction over my eyes to the point that I can't see. I'm grunting as loudly as I can through the small, silk-covered oral orifice and holding a Spanish sign about the Children's Tent Crusade, which will be held in the parking lot behind me.

> People say, "If everything goes according to Hoyle." Who is this Hoyle and why is he in charge? I do not remember voting for anyone other than myself to be the leader of the free world. Especially a guy name Hoyle!
>
> *Mike G. Williams*

Twenty minutes into this experience, I begin to feel a little light-headed. Do you remember the model airplane glue feeling when you were a kid? I'm staggering back and forth, which makes the children laugh hysterically. I'm suffocating inside the bear suit, but I can't tell them I need help, because I can't say "help" in Spanish. Finally, I wander incoherently into the street and am immediately sideswiped by a motor scooter. Now, I'm horizontal on the road as the children are laughing and thinking I'm the funniest thing since the Ricky Martin Bloopers Video. *When I woke up later that evening*, I realized that I would need to learn a few Hispanic phrases if I was going to be of any help in the future. The first phrase being, "Quitame este defrase de oso sudado, antes de que me vuelve loco y pise un nino pequeno." I believe this literally means, "Get this sweaty bear suit off of my body before I go berserk and pummel a small child!"

In my right mind, I would never pummel a small child! *In that overheated condition, however, I would have pled temporary insanity quicker than the Menendez brothers.* Ultimately, I survived and I can laugh about the incident today. What is the spiritual application, you ask? Hmmm, I think… never wear a bear suit in the hot Dominican sun. That's not real spiritual, but it is good advice!

Sometimes we find ourselves in, way over our heads. Not just in a foreign

> I was trying to say "Chief, It is a privilege to be in your beautiful village today and view the rare spider monkeys!" But in my horrible Spanish I announced to the village, "Your Chiefs recent bout with diarrhea has caused the village to smell like a monkey spinkter!" They did not find it as funny as the rest of my mission team.
>
> *Mike G. Williams*

land or language, but in life. There are days when I feel that I'm staggering from side to side and can't find the shade. Still, I can always call on the King. I can call in any language, and He hears and answers. *It takes a big man (or woman) to ask for help.* Unfortunately, that is probably why I often wait until the last minute to cry out. It takes overcoming the cellulite of pride with the muscle of humility. The safest hands will always be that of the Creator. Unfortunately, when I do reach the point that I am willing to ask for help, I usually vocalize it first to people as ill-equipped as myself and not to Him. *I'm not the sharpest tool in the shed.*

> Refrain from judging a man by *what he says* until you find out *why he said* it.
> *Gordon Douglas*

Let's be honest...life happens! You are going along just fine and the next thing you know you are up to your ankles in that which you didn't want to be up to your ankles in. "Com-pren-de Senior?" I encourage you to call out for help today. There is no great valor in dealing with your problems alone. Whatever situations in which you find yourself, dial the help line. Give that situation to the Lord and wait for His miracle. Learn His language... prayer. Try it out today.

In my distress I called upon the Lord my God, and His ears heard my voice. The earth trembled with his response!
Psalms 18:6-7

The Road Less Traveled Is Often Made of Gravel!

My Father often placed my Slip-N-Slide on the gravel driveway.
He believed it would teach me that although life could often be
fun—it was also quite often painful! He was right, and I have
the scars to prove it... scars from life that is.

Mike G. Williams

*H*as anybody thought about making a remote control that really
works? One that does not have controls so small that a hypodermic
needle is needed to trigger the tiny, soft touch buttons? Do we really need
all these useless buttons? *Hey, my VCR still blinks twelve!* Do you think I am
going to do advanced programming on a micro-gizmo control that works
less frequently than a ten-year-old Clapper? I seriously doubt it! I recently
saw one of those "big-button" remote controls they make for seniors. They
must weigh five pounds. *Can seniors even lift one of those puppies?* Just
because it's big, does not mean that I will understand the programming
features any better. I went to school for electronics, but that was in the
eighties! Back then, advanced technology was a four-slot bagel toaster!
Times have changed.

I sat on the couch this morning and watched James Robison and his
wife on television, which is something I often do during my mid-morning
break. I know that taking a mid-morning break seems relatively lack-
adaisical for a guy who doesn't get up until 7 am; but, nevertheless, I do.
Before you get too indignant, let us remember that I usually finish my day
about 1:30 am, so put your judgmental remarks back in the box! James
and his wife were doing one of their mission shows focusing on the little

children around the world being fed by L.I.F.E. International. I enjoy seeing what God is doing through this global ministry. In the midst of my watching, I needed to turn up the volume. This inability to hear quite clearly seems to occur more often with each passing birthday. My wife often shouts from the kitchen, "Turn the television down! Are you going deaf in there?" To which I usually reply, "What, what did you say?" *I actually hear her, but I so enjoy being an annoyance too.* This particular morning, however, I reached for the remote once again to turn it up a notch or two.

> Minnesota is a great place to live, except for the cold. Of course, that's like saying, the sun is a great place to live, except for the heat.
> *Daren Streblow*

As I pushed that rubberized "up" arrow, I watched the channel indicator climb by one digit. I had hit the wrong button and found myself on channel three rather than channel two. Because the batteries in my remote our always low, (Terica says from over-clicking) a lengthy process usually ensues, trying to get the remote working again. *I shake it, bang it against the arm of the recliner, then I twist the batteries back and forth.* As I worked on getting the remote to return to James and Betty, I focused on a PBS show. Channel three is our local PBS affiliate and is one of the most-watched channels in our house. I do let them watch some of the Christian programming, but I have to be careful! The last thing I need is for them to learn about *seed faith* with my credit card The PBS show was called *The Road to Wealth*, if memory serves me correctly. Suzie Orman was the host of this show. I'm sure you have seen her before. I like Suzie, and Suzie gives some great advice, most of it being good common sense. Unfortunately, "common sense" is not an everyday occurrence in most people's lives; however, in her defense, I have often heard Suzie mention that along with the wealth achieved, one could do many great charitable and philanthropic things. Enough said!

Yet, as I watched a little of the "wealth" show, I was able to resuscitate the remote and click back to more of James and Betty's mission program. I couldn't help but have a sense of loss for the many who will gain great wealth in this world, but never share it. It seems ironic that I could watch a show portraying children with bloated bellies, and feel sorry for those who are driving the Lamborghinis. Yet, I do. The mission of L.I.F.E. International also, most certainly, moves me; however, I am concerned for the rich, with good reason. You see, most of my friends are rich in comparison to the rest of the world. *Certainly rich compared to the little children I see on the screen right now.* The scripture clearly points out that the way in which we invest our money on this side of the grave, will determine our rewards on the other side of the grave. I certainly would hate to *"trade the heavenly farm"* for seventy years of exorbitant house payments, only to be living in a tent for the next millennium. Some of you might say, "But Jesus went to build a mansion for me." I realize the John chapter fourteen verse (KJV) said "mansion," but let us remember the Greek word translated "mansion" actually means "room."

Maybe this is the acid test, I don't know. I'm only speculating about this. Perhaps the difference between those who spiritually get it and those who don't, can be easily determined by what motivates them to release their money. Is their life about giving or getting? Is their life about sharing what they have received or hoarding what they have been given? I often jokingly say, "I'm a giver…well, my Doctor says I'm a carrier…but, hey…either way!" Maybe it's not—"either way." The believer has been called to be a giver. In addition, we have been called to be carriers also. We carry the water to the thirsty within our grasp, and we support (give to) the ones who carry the water to those outside of our grasp. This is the manner in which we "lay up treasure" for the day we stand before the throne of God to be judged for the works we have done for Him, with Him, and through Him. I pray that you and I can stand on that day having been great givers and extravagant carriers. Will you be rewarded? Do your own math here. Eternity is not the time to let the accountant give you a report. *By the way, I sent a check to L.I.F.E. today… have you?*

> We are not pro-life because we are warding off death. We are pro-life to the extent that we are men and women for others, all others; to the extent that no human flesh is a stranger to us; to the extent that we can touch the hand of another in love; to the extent that for us there are no "others."
>
> *Brennan Manning*

For God is not unrighteous to forget your work and labor of love, which ye have showed toward his name, in that ye have ministered to others, and continue to do so.
Hebrews 6:10

15

They Need To Invent Oral Duct Tape

Our lives are not determined by what happens to us, rather by how we react to what happens to us. So arm yourselves with automatic weapons and wear a bullet-proof vest!

Mike G. Williams

*M*y wife hates my driving. She trusts me because of my accident-free experience, but mostly she prays often and takes a few Rolaids tablets when we go on a road trip. If it were not for the fact that she hates to fly, we would probably take fewer road trips. I want to drive to the Grand Canyon next summer. Just think of it! Forty-eight hours of delightful high-speed meandering across this beautiful country of ours, only to see a huge hole in the ground, take a few pictures to prove to our friends that we did it, visit the Imax Theater, and start the trip toward home. My dear, sweet wife wants no part of this trip. I can't blame her.

My wife is a nervous passenger. Not a "control-freak" passenger like her husband, who enjoys vicariously navigating from any seat in the vehicle no matter who is driving. She has legitimate concerns. She worries about the

> I could never live on the Space Station, because when I travel I always forget something really important. I can just see myself up there realizing I forgot the water or oxygen bottles.
>
> *Rich Praytor*

62

actions of other drivers, my actions, the actions of pedestrians, and the actions of wild animals. She even worries about the actions of the smallest of all creatures. Yes, I will never forget the day when, in a fit of nervous emotion, she yelled, "Slow down, a bug might run out in front of you!" She meant it! Well, she meant that I should slow down because a squirrel could run out into the street; however, as her tongue began to articulate those words, a big juicy bug hit the windshield, splat! Her mind combined the intended thoughts and the visual "splatting" experience into the now infamous line around our house, "Slow down, a bug might run out in front of you!" We have not stopped laughing about that verbal blunder in many years. Even now a smile is across my face as I remember the moment and type out the memory.

Did she have a Freudian slip? I don't think so. A Freudian slip would be more like having the desire to say something nice but, actually, blurting out something crossing your mind instead. For example, you are eating dinner at the family re-union, and as you attempt to say, "Please pass the potatoes," you unintentionally blurt out, "I hate you! You have all ruined my life! I wish I was never born into this family!" There, now you more fully understand Freudian psychology! I realize that I have oversimplified this a bit. And I'm sorry if that illustration brought up any painful childhood situations. *Seek help.* Really!

> Last time we planned a trip to Puerto Rico my wife asked me if we could drive instead of fly. That cracked me up!
> *Justin Fennell*

If I only had a dollar for every time I said something that I didn't mean to say, I would own that BMW M-class convertible I have been praying for. It would be paid in full, and I would have cash in the trunk. I have to constantly bite my tongue to keep from having to "eat my words." This is tough for a man who makes his living speaking, and most of those words being off the top of his head. I have had a few blunders in my professional life, as well. I believe the tongue is the most-wicked weapon in the arsenal of injury one person can wield. Unfortunately, most tongues are often manned by a quick-tempered unbridled brain, or fueled by deep-seated hurts of the heart. That is a dangerous mix of fertilizer and fuel oil in the hands of a mad man.

Be careful! The enemy of our soul would love to control our tongue. The tongue is so quick in its cutting and so efficient in its energy usage.

Be careful! Think before you speak. Consider the damage that can be done, damage that can take years to overcome. *Duct tape!* Consider it!

Be careful of the power of your tongue. It may appear to be small, but it can fuel a raging forest fire.
James 3:5-6

Somebody Has
Got To Win

Only those who see the invisible can do the impossible. But be careful not to tell others about your ability to see the invisible or you may wind up doing the impossible in a padded room.

Mike G. Williams

*M*y son wants to drop out of T-ball. You see he went to his first game today. Up until now he has just gone to practice. In practice everyone stays very busy catching, throwing, and batting. The game, however, is very different. At the games you find yourself standing on the field waiting for everybody on the other team to get up to bat. Nobody strikes out! So...it can go on for a long time. What angered him was the fact that nobody won. "Everybody gets two times at bat and then you go home. That's no real game, there has to be a winner," my son exclaimed. "Somebody has got to win!" T-ball is designed to teach teamwork and acceptance. My son is a bit more competitive than most. *He really does not get that from me.* For him, there has to be a winner and a loser. Even if he is the loser, he wants the scorecard read out loud. He believes that somebody has got to win.

Somebody has got to win. That is the new slogan for the Florida lottery. I don't know what your feeling on the lottery is; but, personally, I can think of a number of better "bets" in which to invest. *Martha Stewart stock may be one of them. Maybe even Worldcom?* You could invest in comedy videos and CD's. I know this really funny guy who needs a good investor! Not me, of course. I would never use my influence in a self-serving way; you know that. *But since you brought it up, you could go ahead and mail me a check!* I guess my main problem with the lottery is that it plays on the hopes of the downtrodden. I wonder how many little kids will go without milk because Mommy took a gamble… and lost. I am also bothered by the "something for nothing" mentality that has swept our country. But hey, if God has given you the freedom to play it, make sure you give Him ten percent. Dig? Let me move on.

Today our local news did a story on a million-dollar winning lottery ticket that went unclaimed today. 05-24-39-41-46-50 was the number, so you may want to check your wallet. It was purchased in Seminole County on April 21. To date, there have been eighteen unclaimed Florida lottery tickets. That seems ultra ridiculous to me. Seriously, if you are going to play, shouldn't you at least check to see if you've won? That's just my opinion. *I could be wrong.* Hey, give me the five bucks, and I will give you a hug…on the spot! Instant gratification! No more waiting for a *non-forthcoming* reward. I get five bucks, and you get a big sweaty hug from me! Bonus! Somebody has got to win! This way we both win.

> Adversity builds character, but a life of ease does not, think about that next time you take up hang gliding.
> *Al Fike*

Jesus tells us a story about a man who finds a treasure in a field. He then goes and sells everything he owns in order to purchase the field. *Is this insider information?* Good question! Now, because of this investment, he is wealthy enough to have his own television show. *There I go thinking about Martha Stewart again.* My therapist believes it is due to my doily fetish. Many possible scenarios exist in this story. The man could have found the treasure and excitedly jumped up and down shouting, "Treasure, treasure, look what I found!" At that point the guy who owned the field would have promptly asked him to leave the property in order to retrieve the treasure for his own coffers. He could have asked the owner of the land for a price and found that the price was more than he could afford or was willing to pay. He could have shrugged his shoulders, complaining about how people like him can never get ahead. He could have told the owner about the treasure, hoping to receive a small reward. He doesn't, though.

I can imagine in my mind that the man found the treasure and buried it again. I have no idea what he was doing that would cause him to be snooping around in another man's field; Jesus does not tell us. I can see him as he casually runs to the owner's house and negotiates a price for that "worthless old piece of ground that you never use anyway." He may even bargain back and forth for a good deal. I can see him giving the man a deposit in earnest. I can picture him as he goes home and has a garage sale or two…maybe not a garage sale, but, at least, a tent sale. *They did not have many garages back then.* He hardly dares to tell his wife, in fear that the grape vine may give away his secret. I think he may have had to borrow money from a friend, who thinks he is crazy for buying that worthless piece of swampland. Finally, with shekels in hand, he signs his name to the papyrus deed. He probably had a shovel in the trunk of his chariot as he heads out to the property. "The skeptics will see," he says to himself. He may wonder to himself if *even now* he should tell his wife about the treasure. She may want to blow the cash at the

> Don't allow the fear of the unknown to cause you to miss out on what God wants to do through you. Worse than failure is living with the regret of having never stepped out in faith to pursue your vision.
>
> *Andy Stanley*

local mall on trinkets and shiny things. Or worse yet, new clothes for the kids. *This man understands women!* He has in mind a new boat with an outboard motor, a big screen television, and a new air-conditioned camel. Yeah, the important stuff!

Here we have it, the great parabolic comparison. *I don't know if "parabolic" is a real word, but it sounded really theological, so I used it.* What is the value of the treasure that Jesus spoke of? His parallel was definitely a comparison of gusto life with eternal life. When you understand that mankind spends its seventy years looking for just such a thing, you can begin to understand the value. Think about this…we all (everyone) spend (value) our most important asset (time) looking for *real life.* We all invest the farm, shoot the wad, barter the business, and sell the cow in order to get those magic beans called *real life!* In light of that, what kind of treasure are you raising the capital for? Is it something really worth the price you are paying? This question haunts me every single day. You see, I have spent far too many days trying to acquire something I really never wanted. Have you?

I believe the Jesus treasure offer still stands today. I believe that God has hidden great treasure for those who are willing to search for it. Not only search for it, but for those who are willing to pay the price. I can't begin to tell you what this means to you today. What field has the Holy One quietly asked you to "risk it all" to purchase? Maybe it's the calling to a ministry position that will cost you the current, high-paying job. Maybe it's the selling of the family dream home so that you might own a smaller home and give the remainder for a charitable cause. Maybe it is a calling to leave the security of your suburban home for a *third world* mission field. Maybe it is the calling to serve as the janitor at a homeless shelter. Maybe it will require taking less overtime, so you can volunteer at a Hospice. Maybe it is giving up watching football, so you can take your daughter through a "Hooked on Phonics" course. Maybe it is giving up the weekends with friends so that you can spend time developing the character of your son.

Take a minute to ask yourself a question. *Take more than that!* Take a month and inquire of God as to the gravity of the question. *What is real treasure?* What will bring eternal satisfaction and eternal reward? Will you pay the price? Or will the prize go unclaimed? Real life has no lucky numbers. There are, however, educated investments that pay off in the long run. Where is your investment? Where is your risk?

The whole life deal is like a hidden treasure. A wise man will surely trade his meager pittance to gain it.
Matthew 13:44

Some gene pools need to be drained, or at least highly chlorinated!

A verbal contract isn't worth the paper it's written on.

Samuel Goldwyn

I must say that I am not very good at presiding over formal, liturgical, or even, scripted wedding ceremonies. I fly best by the seat of my pants! *Which, by the size of my pants, offers me much room for error.* Yet, I am here again at another wedding, filling in for a pastor who was smart enough to say he was going to be "out of town that weekend." I was handed the ceremony in manuscript form by our Senior Pastor, told to read it, and act interested. Read it and act interested? For a person with ADD, this is a quite a task. I get bored, fidgety, and distracted very easily. I don't pay attention extremely well either. My only salvation is the fact that I can read out-loud at about a gazillion words per minute. That may be a slight exaggeration. This was a talent I developed in school to annoy teachers who would have me read in public. Before you applaud my linguistic skills, let me append the previous statement to include the fact that my speed-reading comprehension is zero!

So here I am at a wedding…again, wearing the much-hated Polyester suit, bored to tears with a less-than-spectacular ceremony that I really don't even

> The President has kept all of the promises he intended to keep.
>
> *George Stephanopolous*
> aide to President Clinton

want attributed to me (all the while, trying to read it and act interested). I'm trying to read it slowly and with heart-felt emotion, and my only sincere thought is that these two probably shouldn't be getting married to begin with. *The pastor may have pawned them off on me, so he would not break his record of having never performed a wedding that ended tragically in murder.* In this case, the most tragic circumstance would be that these two people procreate. I'm sure you understand what I mean. *Some gene pools need to be drained, or at least highly chlorinated!*

I'm reading along fairly well, and I am even acting interested, until I get to the ring ceremony. This is the moment! *My mind is distracted as I try not to humorously insert the phrase "cubic zirconium" before the word "ring."*

> Learning to speak in several different languages is not nearly as valuable as learning to keep your mouth shut in one.
>
> *Farmers Almanac*

While concentrating on not being distracted by this distraction, I had a slight verbal slip-up. I said, "Please take the ring and place it on the third hand of the bride's left finger." The crowd roared with laughter. Realizing what I had done, I said with a southern accent, "And if you can actually do that, I can pronounce you cousins too!"

If I had a dollar for every time I put my foot in my mouth, I would own the Trump Towers. Not only can I read faster than I can comprehend, but I can usually speak much faster than I can think. There is no telling how twisted this book would be if I could type as fast as I think. My lack of typing skills in this case has become an asset to me. A friend once told me that it is better to close one's mouth and be considered an idiot, rather than to open one's mouth and be proven one! I agree.

Silence has never been my golden gift, however. What about you? I much too often find myself filling the air with meaningless trivia and sarcastic remarks that offer about as much encouragement as Boss Hogg offered the Duke boys. I really need to watch what I say. If anyone knows the power of words it should be me. I'm given a platform every time someone asks about my day. I am invited to create opportunities for the kingdom with every question. Utilizing those opportunities comes harder for me than one might think. That old, nasty neighbor, pride, sneaks in and often keeps me from becoming the Evangelist that we are all called to be.

Most of us fear becoming one of those obnoxious, Bible verse quoting, hyper-spiritual, read this pamphlet, run the other way... here they come, extra-spiritual antagonists. You know what (and who) I mean. Maybe you had one of those aunts who could turn a, "How do you make these brownies so moist?" into a twenty minute dissertation on how that "all the professional sports figures and people who watch them are going to hell in a hand-basket." But in reality, not only did she make some great brownies; she kept the most important things of life in front of our faces. I sure miss her, even if she was a little "over-the-top" at times.

My grandfather had a unique way of bringing the light of Christ to any occasion. Whether he was airing-up a tire or ordering a salad at Denny's, my grandfather could find a way to remind us of God's love. It was so easy for him to just slip a good word in here and there. *I want that gift!* I want to have my words peppered with the salt of the Word. I believe his secret depended on the fact that he was so completely immersed in the daily reading of the Word, that it was the natural outpouring of his conversations. Let me repeat myself…daily immersion in the *Word* caused the natural outpouring of the *Word* his conversations. Hmmm, sounds like a simple solution: get into the Word more than I get into the news, sports shows, or even Entertainment Tonight. My friend Herman Bailey is known for closing his television show by saying, "Read two chapters in the Word, and pray for at least ten minutes each day. It will change your life!" Now there is some really great wisdom. Why don't you close this book (I know that will not be difficult) and read a few pages of the Living Book today. The words you read will change the words you say.

> Read two chapters in the Word, and pray for at least ten minutes each day. It will change your life!
>
> *Herman Bailey*

I desire that the words of my mouth and the meditations of my heart to be pleasing and acceptable to our Holy Father.
Psalms 19:14

Raising Rabbits for Fun and Profit

Civilization began its downhill path the day some guy first uttered the words, "A man's gotta' do what a man's gotta' do."

George Carlin

J had just made a semi-illegal left turn out of the mall parking lot. There, on the right side of the road, I noticed a business venture that I never dreamed would have ever existed. We have all seen those unique business opportunities, such as, raising rabbits for fun and profit, addressing envelopes for $3000 a day, or writing your own book (you're reading it). This business opportunity, however, took the cake! It was a big truck with shoes painted all over it. The lettering proclaimed "Mobile Shoe Repair Service." C'mon people, do we need a mobile shoe repair? Are we really having massive blowouts in our high heels that require roadside service? *I'm really tempted to make a "toe"-truck joke right now.* At what point did someone say, "I think a mobile shoe repair would be a great business start up?" Who did the demographics on this one? I doubt they are still in business today.

Not everything is a deluxe idea! Just because you get a new idea, does not mean that it is a good one. We can all think of certain things that really never needed to be invented. Need I mention the Intelligent Clapper? The Flow-bee hair cutting system? Disco? MTV? Erkel? *I think not.* I once invested my life savings (about two-hundred dollars at the time) in a bunch of gold-tone pendant watches. They all worked for about a week and then, as if they were programmed, quit working. I was devastated. So were my customers! That year everyone in my family got broken gold-tone pendant watches for Christmas. I told them that they were non-working antique watch replicas. *I don't think they bought my explanation.*

My communication with God is often quite the same. There are days when "I" get this great idea and I proclaim, "This is what God wants me to do!" Time soon points out the error of my ways, and I find myself on my knees asking God how I could have missed His will so badly. There are other times when I feel as if I can hear His voice, and I choose to write it off as a fluke, only to find out that I missed a great opportunity to partner with the great Creator. I fall down and I mess up and I miss the boat and I often rebel against the Plan. I am truly an idiot at times. God is so longsuffering with my stupidity and hard headedness. I'm very thankful for His grace and mercy. *But mostly grace, no make that mercy, no you better make that grace.*

As a believer in Christ, I am daily walking in the grace and mercy of God. I realize that I could never do anything to deserve or earn His grace or mercy, but still He gives it. That is a good thing. That is a precious thing! Let me remind you to stay on your face before God in prayer and scripture reading. The writing of these little devotionals has caused me to be challenged in my own spiritual walk. I have been challenged in areas that I cannot, at this time, even write about because I am still processing. Maybe in Turkey Soup Volume Four, subtitled…Mike Finally Comes Clean.

> I don't understand why they make you wait at the speaker box to hear your total before driving around to the second drive-thru window. Are there really people who need to hear the total first, so they can be saving up the money before they get to the second window? "Alright fellow passengers… let's not be spending any money unnecessarily before we get around to the second window. We are going to need three dollars when we finally get there!"
>
> *Mike G. Williams*

The Apostle Paul reminds us, "Do not use your liberty (grace experienced) as permission to serve your fleshly desires." Wow, strong words from a man who fully understood the struggles of following the King to the maximum. Paul understood that we all have the tendency to grow

> Anyone who has never made a mistake has never tried anything new.
>
> *Albert Einstein*

complacent, lazy, apathetic, and lethargic. We all have the tendencies to sneak back to taste again that with which we were most familiar. Unfortunately, some of us allow the "grace of God" to be stretched to the max. It does stretch! But be careful! Let us, who have been called in grace, walk worthy of that grace because of our great love for the Savior.

All things are lawful for me but all things are not great ideas! I have the freedom to participate in many activities, but I must be careful not to become controlled by those activities.
1 Corinthians 6:12

Double Standards
for the Pilots

If it is illegal to yell "FIRE!" in a crowded theater... It should be illegal to yell "THEATER!" at a fire. That's just my opinion.

Mike G. Williams

OK, I'm on a plane, and I'm sure I smell cigarette smoke, right? I'm waiting for the pilot to come out, break in the lavatory with a razor-sharp axe, immobilize the perpetrator with a zap from a stun gun, secure him with wire ties, and slap that sucker with a five-hundred-dollar fine for disabling a lavatory smoke detector. Maybe the passengers can take turns beating him, or her (it could be a lady in there). Maybe this smoker can be sentenced to flying the rest of his life with a seat that won't recline or a non-working air conditioning vent. Suddenly, the lavatory door bursts open, and out walks an eight-year-old girl, who doesn't smell at all like smoke. Hmmm, this is a little unnerving.

Call me silly, but I don't like to smell smoke on airplanes. Usually, this particular odor is a precursor to trouble! *Just ask the Leonard Skynerd Band...well, if you could.* I, therefore, nonchalantly mentioned to the flight attendant that I smelled smoke. She discretely whispered to me, "The pilot is having a quick smoke." Hey! What do you mean, "The pilot is having a smoke" and we can't? Not that I would want to do this practice anyway.

> I just flew in here... boy are my arms tired!
>
> *Henny Youngman*

Nevertheless, as an American, I don't like to be told the "I-can't-do-something-that-someone-else-can!" *Did that make any sense at all?* She informed me that, although it is illegal to smoke in the aircraft passenger compartment or lavatory, it is legal to smoke in the pilot's compartment. Hmmm…do I smell smoke…or double standards, here? Then I considered the implications of pilots going through nicotine fits while trying to land a plane. I would hate to think that what seemed like a turbulent landing was actually *Captain Kirk* having a nicotine withdrawal.

Admittedly, I hold double standards for myself in a few places (small places, insignificant places, of course). I respect my own personal right to eat with unwashed hands; although, I demand to see some toweling action when the fast-food worker is coming out of the bathroom door. I don't mind running a little over the speed limit myself, but don't you dare pass me… I would consider you to be driving *way* too fast! Watch the way you speak to me; but please, forgive my speech, especially in a crisis situation. Hey, I was stressed. I just said what came natural to me. *Hmmm, yes natural.*

> Is a vegetarian allowed to eat animal crackers?
> *George Carlin*

There is one place that you will never get away with double standards. Kids! Yes, kids! Those little inquisitors of the known world, kids! Those tiny questioners of all things taken for granted. The ones who dare to innocently ask, "why?" *They are the ones who possess the immaturity to question those of us who are supposed to be mature, asking questions that are way too mature to answer fully.* Notice that I said "fully" and not "truthfully." I am a parent, you know. Children can spot double standards quicker than Inspector #7 can spot a faulty elastic waistband. They are born keen disciples of the "that's-not-fair principle," and it seems to permeate their observations of all things surrounding them.

I wonder how we affect them by our double standards. I'm not talking about allowing them to stay up until twelve when they should have gone to bed at seven. I'm thinking about the other things. Need I mention the television shows we watch or the movies we attend? *I think not.* How did you feel about the double standards of your parents? Their inconsistencies are often crystal-clear in our memories. Should these double standards be the norm? Maybe you are not a parent, but have younger siblings who look up to you. How does your life play out before them? Yikes! God, help me to be an ambassador and representative of unwavering truth! I desire for my life to be an example suitable of following.

You are living letters! Known and read by everybody. Show that you are a letter from Christ.
2 Corinthians 3:2

I.Q. Hunting

We should have a way of telling people they have bad breath without hurting their feelings. "Well, I'm bored, let's go brush our teeth," or, "I've got to make a phone call, would you hold this gum in your mouth for me?"

Brad Stine

For the most part I wouldn't give you a dime for the 24-hour news networks. I think they are jaded and biased and relatively incapable of simply reporting the facts. Perhaps "simply reporting facts" is too much to ask. I don't know that I could just "give you the facts" without offering my commentary on them. May I also say that I am bothered by the way news people "sensationalize" the happenings around the nation. The news is becoming a blend of tabloid sensationalism and Hollywood commentary suitable for nothing more than an immediate click of the remote to a more believable network, *like TV Land!*

In Florida, the newscasters live for a good Hurricane. You can see it in their faces as they try to appear somber while reporting on the "Big Storm" on the horizon. They are excited! It's one of the few big stories that will really keep Floridians glued to the set, other than a piece on Social Security reform issues. *I think you understand.* We did enjoy the whole vote recount thing for a while, but that soon passed and we got back to real life. *We knew the people in South Florida couldn't count years ago.* Remind a South Florida resident that Florida is forty-ninth in education and you're likely to hear, "Out of how many?" Well that or…"no habla Englishey?" I don't mean that in a bad way.

I imagine that if I was a news producer, I would have to include a little more comedy in the mix. It would probably resemble the *Saturday Night Live—Weekend Update.* Unfortunately statistics show that the way many people get their news is from the *comedic recaps* brought to them from the late night talk show monologues. That could be a GOOD thing! If it were my newscast, I would want my reporters to interview some politician, and the moment he makes some off-the-wall statement (lie), they would just start belly laughing. The whole crew could just start laughing! *I would also like the graphics guys to paint mustaches or little red horns on everyone just to spice up the show a little.* That would be funny! We could say, "Tonight's broadcast is sponsored by Captain Morgan!" *Of course, all of my news anchors would be midgets!* It's time they got to work in broadcast news, and DANG IT, I'm the one to help! I care! *I am going on record right now in demanding equal employment opportunities for the vertically challenged!*

Do you ever wish your local news would stop interviewing people who are clueless? You know the ones I'm talking about. Somebody is arrested for some horrible crime, and the camera crews race out to interview an unemployed neighbor from two blocks away who is willing to appear on camera so

> Do unto others as you would have them do unto you. Unless you are a sadist, then it might be best to leave people alone.
>
> *Mike G. Williams*

he or she can spout their idiotic thoughts about nothing in hopes to see themselves on the *"Tee-Veey".* Why do they always seem to find the guy with no shirt, two teeth, a *Bud Light* can in his hand, two *Marlboro's* behind each ear, and one in his mouth? Why must they pick out the guy who was never *hooked on phonics*, or for that matter has not read a book since 1974, and that was *The Idiots Guide to Trailer Park Living?* Why must they choose the one individual who would give an opinion about anything, yet has no pertinent information except…who will be on the *World Wide Wrestling Federation* pay-per-view next Sunday? Can they only find a guy who hasn't shaved since the last election? Can they only find a guy who looks more terrifying than the cannibal they are reporting on? Can they only find a lady whose prideful claim to fame is that she has a tattoo of her mom on her left buttocks that somewhat resembles *David Letterman* with a three day beard?

Oh, they find those sweethearts of the rodeo too! There is the husky lady in the purple tube top three sizes too small, who also hasn't shaved since the Carter administration, and not because she's French! Of course she will have her seven kids in her arms who will hold her cigarette for her while she tries to articulate her analysis of the situation. "Uh, uh, I didn't…uh…have…uh…no idea that…he was…uh…like that…Ever since he'd just got ouwda the jail…uh…he's been a real…swell…neighbor…I used to let my kids stay at his house at night…uh…when I was working late at the Waffle House. I just don't…uh…understand it." Listen to me, Network News People! Quit interviewing people who *don't have A CLUE!* We want information, not lack of it!

Stop interviewing neighbors altogether! *We don't really care what they think!* Unless they are the actual person who reported the crime, they have no relative or applicable knowledge! These child-breeding, mouth-breathing, pit-bull-raising neighbors don't need a forum! These people need counseling! *Long term counseling!* Don't fill news time with quackery. Skip the quackery and give us another *AFLAC* commercial or a Carrot Top 1-800-CALLATT marathon. That way at least the stupidity could be somewhat entertaining.

> When a package says "Open Other End" I purposely open the end where it says that. I will be nobody's slave.
> *Justin Fennell*

Quite possibly the reason for this subjects tirade is because, at the moment, I am sitting in a hotel room watching the strike on Iraq. I'm sure that many of you are watching it too. Although by the time you read this, it will have been long past. Tonight I am at Champions Forest Church in Houston. They have put me here in this swank *French* hotel. The *French* are not in favored status here in Texas right now. I should have known there was something amiss when I entered the lobby and heard the *Dixie Chicks* music playing over the intercom. Nevertheless, they have a television in each room, so here I sit. The FOX network news broadcaster just announced that they were going to break away to the local affiliates for some local news. That's okay. I need to see what is happening on a local level to prepare for the evening concert. To my surprise, when they switched to the local affiliate, we did NOT get local news. Instead, we got an anchorman standing against a green screen, trying to explain with elementary simplicity what we had just seen on the network; all the while, diminishing the intelligence and production quality considerably. He mumbled through simple names and often confused Saddam with Osama. He is used to sitting behind a desk, so standing in front of a map he looks like the *Hunchback of Notre Dame* with Egypt hovering over his right shoulder blade. Then, this local FOX affiliate had the audacity to go to the streets and get some "local opinions," because that's obviously what the public really wants, local redneck experts sharing what they think. *Again they found the dumbest mouth-breathers in the Lone Star State to share their deep insights.* Pertinent comments such as, "Saddam better not try to invade Texas or else," and thought-provoking analysis like, "I think we ought to just bomb the (bleep) out of them." Hey, that's a great idea. I'll bet they never thought about including bombs in the "shock and awe" concept. *Duh!* Call President Bush and give him that info quick! *Our boys certainly need to consider this "bombing the (bleep) out of them" idea!*

I appreciate our soldiers! Whether you agree with the war or not, we appreciate the boys who serve our country. When I say "boys" I certainly mean that in a *gender-neutral* way, not in a *"don't ask—don't tell"* way! I realize there are many wonderful women serving us equally as well. I am thankful for the men and women who serve our military without question. In the midst of loud-mouthed protesters around this country, I am thankful that our soldiers do their job. These soldiers are not nearing Baghdad, deciding to lie down in front of their tanks and burn the flag. They leave the protesting to the people at home who, seemingly, have the time to that. And, those who live in a country where people have fought and died so they could do that!

I am truly thankful for freedom of speech. People should have a right to hit, punch, burn, and destroy property to demonstrate the need for "peace" and other *anti-violent* ideas. I'm sorry, but it bugs me when I see people protest violence with violence and destruction. Despite the protests, our

> A solider on active duty does not become entangled in civilian affairs.
>
> *Missionary Jim Elliot*

boys are in the Jeeps headed toward Baghdad because their Commander and Chief said to go. They may not understand the mission; they may not fully agree with the plan of attack, but they are rolling toward the city as we speak! They may have fears or even feel unprepared, but they roll on with weapons in hand. Why? Because they are soldiers! They have placed themselves under the authority of their leaders and will follow those leaders. This is not to say that they have never questioned their own sanity for joining this *band of brothers*, but that choice is now in the past. When asked about the protestors at home, they have little to say. It is as if the seriousness of their mission at hand is their *only* vision. They roll on.

What a parallel for those of us who seek to follow and serve another Commander and Chief! What an example for those of us who also call ourselves "a band of brothers" united for a cause! What a powerful example of being unmoved by the whims and whines of the critics around me! I am a soldier! I may never march in the infantry, ride in the cavalry, shoot the artillery, or fly over the enemy, but I'm in the Lord's army! *I just could not help remembering that childhood favorite.* I AM in the Lord's army! I was called, chosen, drafted, and I enlisted! I stood before witnesses and pledged my allegiance to the Savior and asked him to be my Commander and Chief. I went through the Boot Camps of Sunday School, Bible School, Discipleship Training, Summer Camp, Seminars, books, and Scripture reading. I am now called to the mission proposed by my Commander and Chief—a mission for which He has equipped me. *I roll on!*

There have been times when I questioned my sanity for joining this band. There have been days where my faith has been shaken. There have been times of depression when I have felt ill equipped for the calling I had been given. Admittedly, it would be much easier if I would receive a *personal* pep talk more often, but I do hold in my hand the history of this Army and a personal letter from the Commander. Therefore, I press on in faith.

Sure, I know that there are dissenters back home. There are always those who will protest and question the Commander's choice of missions, but let them be. I was not called to battle *over the* mission, only to battle *according to* mission. If they choose to bog down in the rights and wrongs of the mission, that is their business. The Commander will deal with them about that personally one day. My goal is to be *on* the mission. I have been asked to go into hostile territory and free an oppressed people from an evil tyrant. This ultimate *"axis of evil"* has been oppressing nations for years. He has enslaved families and killed even the people who serve his cause, making prisoners of war out of those who fell victim to his lies. My job is to go into the city and liberate! I am commissioned to liberate the captive, free the oppressed, and open the eyes of those who have been blinded by years of hopelessness. Well, enough talking about it! I must roll on!

The Spirit of the Lord is upon me and has anointed me to preach the gospel to the poor, heal the broken hearted, bring deliverance to the captives, and restore sight to the blind, and to set free those who are bruised!

Luke 4:18

Recycled Christmas Trees

Everybody is somebody else's wacko... even me... but especially you!

Mike G. Williams

*M*ost of you know that I have served time. Seven long years to be exact! *As a youth director!* "Served time" sounds as if I were referring to prison, doesn't it? No, "prison" is not a true description of time spent with a youth group. It might, however, be a correct metaphor if I were referring to a music director's job. Youth directing is an interesting life. It combines the skills of a certified counselor with that of a high school volleyball coach. Chauffeuring is a must! Some wood-shop skills and auto mechanics are important; and, of course, one needs to be keeping up with the latest trends. You need to know the Bible, as well as MTV, the latest styles, magazines, movies, and pizza. Being "cool" is not a necessity, but being easy to talk to, is. *Of course, you need to do all this while supporting yourself and family on a very meager paycheck.*

One of your jobs is to create new and interesting games for the students to play during the various activities you have planned. The idea (in the minds of the parents, at least) is to keep the students so busy, that they do not have time to think about (or participate in) sinful things. Over the years, therefore, I have come up with some fairly creative ways of doing fun and time-filling activities *cheaply*. Cheaply always being the accepted mode of operation because, although we want to do the best job for the kids, we want to do it on a shoestring budget. So...weird and cheap creativity was always the priority of the day.

One of my favorite events was the Annual Christmas-Tree-Recycling Party. Sometimes we would have two or three of these annual events immediately following the sacred season. We would go around collecting old, dead Christmas trees from front lawns before the garbage men could snag them. We would recycle each tree; meaning, we would put it in the van with us, or on the roof, and then take it to someone else's house and put it on their front lawn. Some nights we would bring as many as twenty-five old trees to an unsuspecting stranger's home. Other times we would simply take the tree from the road where it had been placed for pick-up, and place it back on that person's front porch with a note that stated, "Due to this year's live-tree-disposal restrictions, you will be required to keep this tree and dispose of it next year." We would always create some official-looking letterhead similar to that which may be used by "official-types" of the town, the county, or, of course, *Green Peace*. The teens loved sneaking up to the house of a staff pastor or deacon with twenty-five trees. They also enjoyed taking videos of each other "in the act." It usually started out as a "church-member-only" event, but kind of broadened its way to include whomever we thought needed our type of little "blessing." Sometimes it was a noisy neighbor, an expensive house, or maybe a *Jewish* family! *The Jewish families dearly loved seeing Christmas trees stacked at their houses to celebrate the season.* One time we even set up a manger scene in front of my attorney's home! He doesn't work for me anymore. You have to have cheap fun where you can!

> It bothers me that the lettuce on a Whopper taste like it was washed in discarded medical waste.
>
> *Bryan Scheer*

Then there was the Annual Tree Burning. Although we firmly believed in recycling, global warming and air pollution was not a great concern back then. We would gather a few trees and recreate a scene from The Towering Inferno, all the while singing Christmas songs and roasting hot dogs and marshmallows on unfolded coat hangers. By far, the most exiting Christmas had to be the year that we decided to have a "tree toss." *Probably the most dangerous of all the games, the "tree toss" may have played a part in my retiring from full-time youth work completely.* The sport resembled something you would expect to see at the Redneck Olympics. The seats would be removed from a van and teams of two would be chosen. Each team would place four discarded Christmas trees into the side door of the van. Four garbage cans had been strategically placed along the church driveway. The van would reach a speed of 30 M.P.H. as the teams would attempt to heave the trees out of the side door of the moving vehicle and knock over the garbage cans. The team that successfully knocked down the most cans was the winner Of course, we had tournaments, so the game could last for hours with variations of the same theme. The danger level and the uniqueness of the sport made it a thrill for everyone, although the joy of the game was somehow lost when I was called in to explain it to the board.

> I had a friend once who said she would never go to Hawaii because she said, "they hate Americans over there."
> *Tim Hawkins*

As the years progressed, so did the variations on this "recycled tree" theme. Our last game variation (well, the last game variation before I was—shall we say—laid-off from my job at the church) was the Burning Christmas Tree Toss. Yes, I used the word "burning." It was the job of each team to set their tree on fire without the use of accelerants! *Well...none that we knew of!* They would tie a piece of rope to the tree trunk, light the branches on fire, swing it round and round like David's sling-shot, and release the tree into the air. The tree that flew the farthest was the winner. We would videotape the event in order to re-watch each one for a second chance at winning "visual presentation." It was a stunning event that combined sight, sound, and just enough *extreme danger* to make it absolutely fabulous! I hope to see it at the X-games next year.

I have always loved trees. I remember as a kid, almost living in them. I was a tree climber! *I wanted to be a member of the Swiss Family Robinson's family until I was about thirty-two!* Even to this day, I really enjoy flying into the Great Northwest, if for nothing more than seeing the enormous trees. Most of the time as I fly over towns, I see big buildings and little trees standing next to them. In Portland, one sees the big buildings and the even bigger trees towering above them. They just appear so gigantic to this Florida boy. Like something you would see on a sci-fi movie involving Japanese tree cloning. I can see it now, *Attack of the Killer Redwoods* coming to a theater near you!

Intriguing, isn't it, how trees grow so big in such a cold, harsh climate, when I can't seem to get the trees in my Florida yard to climb over ten feet.

Even when I fertilize them with my neighbor's cats, they don't seem to grow. *Take that last comment any way you want to.* I recently watched the PBS special on trees. It explained how a tree has to have wind to grow stronger. It seems that the wind pushing against these trees causes *tree muscles* (I don't think that is the official term) to build strength and make the tree stronger. They proved this using one of these biosphere scientific bubble experiments. The trees grown inside the biosphere bubble, where there was no wind, were weak, soft, and in poor health. Can you make the correlation?

Do you think God designed *wind* to make us stronger too? Good question! Maybe our wind is a different kind of wind. Does resistance build our spiritual muscles? I know that sounds like something you would hear on a Bow-Flex infomercial, but momentarily compare it to the words of St James. He said, "The trying of your faith brings patience to your life." That which causes us to struggle, also causes us to grow! *Interesting concept... I do say.* Maybe that is why

> Pleasure is as difficult to pursue as the end of a rainbow. Look for pleasure and you will never find it. Whenever you try to seize it by the tail, it eludes you...for pleasure is a by-product, a side effect. It takes us by surprise when we are looking for something else. Seek God and you find, among other things, piercing pleasure. Seek pleasure and in the long run you find boredom, disillusionment, and enslavement.
>
> *John White*

James went on to say, "So, let these trials continue to happen that we may become mature, strong, and complete." Maybe it is time I begin to look at resistance (trials) in a different way. Maybe life with all of its *stuff* has been strategically designed for my spiritual health. What do you think? How then will you respond? How then will I respond? Will you greet resistance as an aerobic friend, or fight it as an evil foe? Maybe we should welcome adversity as tool for our growth.

My brothers and sisters, whenever you face resistance of any kind, consider it nothing but joy!
James 1:2a

I Could Never
Be a Priest

The worse thing about living on the Space Station is if you had the ability to levitate... you couldn't prove it to anybody.

Mike G. Williams

J walked into the Biltmore Hotel wearing a *flashy* new suit. It was one of those button-up-to-the-top units. Have you seen them? I know you have? Benny Hinn wears a similarly designed white one on his television show. *And after Labor Day even? The audacity! The fashion faux pas!* Benny looks rather angelic; whereas, biscuit-ous guys (fat men), like me, love these suits for their slimming qualities... although we would not wear white. White clothing tends to make a large guy loom like a water tower against the dark sky. *Biscuit-ous is a term that I have been coining since a lady told me that the space between my pants and my T-shirt reminded her of a tube of freshly opened biscuits.* This particular October evening, however, I found myself at a fundraising event for a Crisis Pregnancy Center. There must have been ten Catholic Priests in the room; every one of them wearing *my* polyester suit! *Well, theirs had the addition of a little white-collar piece.* As I would pass them in the banquet hall, they would eye me up and down as if to telepathically notify me that my collar had obviously fallen off. One inquired to which Parish I belonged, and I responded, "Our Lady of Affordable Entertainment!" We had so much fun with the little costume, that the emcee actually introduced me as Father Mike.

I have to say that the priests took the joke really well. In fact, after the show a few of them inquired about my willingness to come and perform at their next Bingo night. I think they really just wanted to get a greater share of the Protestant gambling market. I think they believe that most of protestant money goes directly to televangelists in exchange for a cheap cassette tape, or a comedy CD. *At least the Catholics offered a chance at a five-hundred-dollar jackpot.* I pretended to be interested in case they happened to mention the phrase, "Large honorarium!" My denominational affiliation *can't* be bought, but it can be rented. For fifty dollars a night, I would be glad to tell jokes between "B-5" and "B-14." Call me a businessman if you must. I have diapers to pay for!

During the evening dinner, I sat next to a funeral director. I must say that he was a hoot. We laughed throughout the entire dinner. During the overcooked chicken cordon bleu, I asked him a question. It was a question that I had thought about a few years before when my Dad and I went to look at caskets for he and mom. I didn't want to make light of the situation when shopping with my dad, but now, I was willing to fire off my question. So…I turned to him and said, "So… the casket sales guy told us that the company would stand behind all of their caskets, and there was a choice of a fifty-year or seventy-five year warranty on each model." That cracked me up—to think that there might be people out there, returning caskets for repair in fifty years. How would you know if one goes bad? They could offer a lifetime warranty if they wanted. *Hey… the guys dead— warranty VOID!* Who would check it? He explained that occasionally they have had to move a body from one cemetery to another, and often find rust on the casket. A loved one could request that it be repaired before the casket was reburied, but only if they had the deluxe warranty package. I said, "Have it repaired? O come on, are they going to send the casket down to Vinnie's Paint & Body Shop for a light sand blasting, rust repair, and repainting?" That is really what I want to hear the next time I go in for a little bodywork! "Hey Father Mike, just pull your wrecked Jeep over next to the rusty coffin." *That's too weird!*

> Concerned medical experts have diagnosed this problem as an epidemic outbreak of…yes, that's right, hypochondria, it's the *all-in-your-head* cold.
>
> *Dennis Miller*

He went on to tell me a number of really cool stories. He said that in days gone by, the local funeral home workers also served as the ambulance operators. If you ask me, this is a conflict of interest. *I really don't need a funeral home director who might be a little short on making payroll this week, responsible for getting me to the hospital quickly.* I can visualize these guys stopping off at the Waffle House while I lay in the back of their meat wagon clutching my chest. That really bothers me! The second-hand smoke from the Waffle House patrons alone could clog what little I had left of a coronary blood flow. Times have changed! We now have skilled EMT's working our emergency situations; and, of course, the occasional young lawyer with a police scanner.

I deal daily with conflict of interest. Even in the effects of writing this book. There is the conflict of writing comedy—versus content. There is the conflict of writing deep theology—versus you buying it. *Okay, Mike Williams writing "deep theology" is a fat-chance, but it could happen.* I have thought about hiring a ghost- writer! So, there you go; the possibility exists. *I wonder if Jerry Jenkins is available?* I am not alone in my battle with conflict. The apostle Paul knew a little about conflict. He described what was going on in his mind as a "war." He intricately detailed his battle with the flesh and declared himself the unfortunate loser at times. He claimed to hold the title of the Chief of Sinners; all the while, directing, shepherding, and leading many a New Testament church, and often from a jail cell. I think he knew conflict in many ways and on multiple sides.

> Why do you hasten to remove anything that hurts your eye, while if something effects your soul, you postpone the cure until next year?
>
> *Horace*

The conflict...well, I should say...one of many conflicts, came about for me many years ago in my own life. I had the ability to make a profit or lose a profit, depending upon the information I revealed to a potential customer. One option was the full truth, and the other was simply the omission of the full truth. I failed, and failed miserably. It was only a few days ago that God brought it to my memory and asked me what I was going to do about it? Of course, I asked for forgiveness, but this was deeper. He was desirous of knowing how really willing I was to make amends. This week I will write a check to that organization. I'm not sure whether or not I will send them any interest though. *Maybe I should* Sometimes it takes me years to come to repentance. I am a slow learner. What about you? Is anything coming to your mind right now? I thought so.

There is a battle going on in our minds. An actual war. CNN, MSNBC, and FOX will not be covering it, but never the less, it still rages. The fight to do what is right compared to doing what is wrong for personal gain strides forward every day. How is your battle coming? *I failed a few times this week.* What stand have your mental soldiers taken? Have you read the battle plan found in the book of God? Have you asked for any help from others? Yes, having someone else pray for me and hold me accountable for a good battle plan is extremely important!

We should please and obey God rather than ourselves.
Acts 5:29

Some People
Bother Me

Telemarketers that call during dinner hours should be flogged with their very own phone and then strangled with the cord.

Mike G. Williams

There are a few different types of people who bother me in this world. I will not bore you with the actual list, especially since this book has a finite number of pages. Okay, maybe I'll just share my top three. Number three has to be the people who bring eleven items into the ten-item/cash only express aisle and then leisurely decide to write a check. Number two would be the phone solicitors who ask, "How you are doing?" Then say, "good" to whatever response they hear, immediately proceeding to read their script. I could have responded, "My foot was amputated earlier this week!" Doesn't matter. They keep right on reading! The "numero-uno" people-group that gets under my skin is the group who give testimonials involving horrible situations that might…could have…possibly…almost…happened if! Let me give you a brief example. Although I will not name any names, this person (we will call her Betty) said, "*Last week my local bank branch was robbed on Wednesday afternoon at 3 p.m. by a guy with a wooden gun. The people didn't know it was a wooden gun at the time, and he robbed the bank of almost ten thousand dollars! I was*

> I believe that having a tattoo on your neck that says "White Trash" is a little redundant!
>
> *Tim Hawkins*

in that same bank on Monday morning, and I just want to offer up praise that I did not go in on Wednesday and, therefore, was not almost killed in that terrible ordeal. When I heard about it I just shook with fear knowing how close I came to losing my life!! I'm shaking even now just telling about this."

I don't want to be critical here; but Betty, you were not close to being involved in a robbery... you and the actual robbery were at least 52 hours apart! Neither were you "close" to being killed! Consider this, the greatest danger was a possible splinter from the *wooden* gun! The chances of that actually happening are comparable to a person getting struck by lightning while simultaneously being attacked by a shark in your bathtub. *Hmmm, that sounds like a close call I don't think has yet been mentioned at prayer/praise time.* Maybe next week. I think Betty ought to share that one; that is, unless you want to use it.

People listen to me; everyday we come within inches of death. Everything from those little microscopic bugs that are burrowing through each of our scalps right now, to the radio transmissions that are rapidly sloshing through our body (my dad always told me that rock music would kill people). It could be from a flash flood, an out of control driver, or a cell phone accident. That's right, you could be hit in the head with a cell phone that someone left on the wing of an airplane, which, after take off, fell from 35,000 feet in the air and came crashing through the roof of your BMW convertible. *Who knew?*

I want to nicely close with this thought: *Get a Life!* Quit trying to live your praise life through vicarious hypothetical close calls. Offer praise for the really great things in life like old-fashioned front porch swings, permission to

> The way people are afraid of the Ten Commandments is so weird. "Get it away, don't hang it here, and don't put it there." You would think it came out of the "ARK OF THE COVENANT" or something... But I guess it IS offensive... especially if you're a liar, adulterer, idol worshipper, a fornicator, or basically any recent guest on the Jerry Springer Show.
>
> *Nazareth*

> Unless you are an Olympic diver, any guy caught wearing a Speedo should be flogged senselessly.
>
> *Mike. G. Williams*

93

take your shoes off, hearing that the tumor was benign, and railroad graffiti that rivals what you might see at a museum. Also, let's not forget permission to keep your shoes on, communion cups big enough to quench your thirst, quick wits, sarcastic friends who make you laugh…and make you think, a child's hug, White Castle Hamburgers, Skyline Chili, and the subsequent Rolaids.

Continuously give thanks to God for everything.
Yes everything!
Ephesians 5:20

This Tub Leaks

I believe if the Limbo was added to the Olympic Games it would give Midgets an unfair advantage.

Mike G. Williams

*T*here are few things you need to have in order to operate a boat in this country. The first is a boat, of course. That goes without saying. The second is the mandatory safety devices such as life preservers, whistle, and lights. Third, you need a boat registration. Also helpful might be a trailer, enabling you to get the boat to water, provided you don't live on water. A good dose of common sense should also be required. *Unfortunately, common sense is not a mandated, legal requirement; although, it should be.*

Weekend boaters are a unique breed They are much more excited and a lot more nervous than the guy who lives on the water. Their excitement tends to cause them to have very little patience, especially at the boat ramp. Let me explain. You have Billy Boater who has waited all week to take his fourteen-foot Little Miss Budweiser Wanna-Be down to the lake for a day of fishing. He spent most of his Friday evening packing up all the gear. He probably spent some time sitting behind the wheel, pretending he was sailing across the water. *More than likely he did this while his kids and wife were not looking.* He laid awake all night in anticipation! By the break of dawn, he is out of the shower and wondering why the rest of his family is not already in the boat. Slightly perturbed, he chides them to get dressed, so they can have a "fun family day" on the water. He learned to call his little quest "fun family day" to appease his conscience for spending too much money on a boat that he only uses four times a year. So...while he is impatiently waiting on the rest of the family, he hops into the boat for one more dream behind the helm. The helm is a nautical term meaning the steering wheel. *He learned this reading a Boaters World magazine at the Barber Shop.* He also learned the words "starboard, port, bow, aft, stern, keel, trim," and a few other words which he will (improperly) use during the day to confuse his family in an attempt to appear nautically savvy.

Upon arrival at the boat ramp, he sees that he is now in line behind three other weekend boaters, who are launching their vessels much too slowly for his liking. With a growl, he jumps out of the car and helps them guide their boats and trailers down to the water's edge in hopes that this will speed up the process. "These are obvious rank amateurs," he mumbles to himself. A long fifteen minutes later, he finds himself backing his little SUV and boat trailer down the ramp. This is done in zigzag fashion, and is often accompanied by loud phrases like "You kids duck down," "I can see the pole dear," and "Will you just shut up and let me concentrate?" Once he gets it to the water, he exclaims, "All right, Honey, you get behind the steering wheel and I will undo the tie-downs, get in the boat, and man the helm! Just back us into the water slowly! I will fire-up the engine and back the boat right off the trailer." He knows that is the way they do it on all the professional fishing shows. How hard can it be? *Orlando Wilson does it every week without incident.* "When the boat is clear of the trailer, you pull forward into the parking space. We'll show these *hokey-pokey wanna* be skippers how it is supposed to be done," he shouts with arrogant pride.

His impatience is now at its prime. What was supposed to be a 7 a.m. launch is now two hours late. As his wife backs the boat into the water,

> I go to a huge church. It's so crowded they've started putting up those amusement park ropes outside the sanctuary to control the crowd between services. There's a sign at the end that says, "You are now forty-five minutes from the sermon."
>
> *Robert G. Lee*

he lowers the engine and reaches for the key switch. Woops, the key is not in the ignition. "Wait," he yells, "Where's the key?" *It is too late, however.* The boat is now halfway off the trailer from the backwards inertia of the vehicle Bobbing up and down in the water, the boat bangs its fiberglass hull against the steel trailer frame. He realizes the key is on the float ring in the glove box and, waving wildly, yells for his wife throw it to him quickly. Recognizing his wild motions as a signal to pull away, she drops the car into first gear and…*BANG*… a chunk of fiberglass is ripped from the nose of the boat, as the trailer impacts it coming out of the water. Boat Boy is now waving his hands like Tom Hanks in that movie. You know the one. *The one where he waves his hands at the rescue planes. I can't remember the name of it, but it was the one where he named the volleyball Wilson.* Seconds drag by like hours, as "boat-man" graciously, of course, communicates the problem, while the poor wife frantically digs through the glove box. Finally she appears at the side of the vehicle and throws the keys. They bounce off the bow and into the water. As he climbs to the front of the boat, trying to retrieve the floating keys, he becomes aware of a slight problem. Unbeknownst to him, the drain plug had been left out of the rear transom. The drain plug is a little rubber and brass item similar to what they used in the old claw-foot bathtubs. It allows any water in the hull to be drained when the boat is not in the water. While the boat is IN the water, however, removing this plug would be tantamount to cutting a small hole in the bottom of the boat. *Not a good idea, Skipper. Didn't the SS Minnow start out like this?* While our boating buddy was extremely concerned with getting the family fun day started, he had overlooked the importance of having a vessel that stayed afloat!

Well, our friend finally found the key. He used an empty tackle box to bail out most of the water. It wasn't the best day he ever had. They say that the two best days of your life are the day you buy a boat, and the day you sell it. *My Dad sold the boat at the end of the summer. And do you know what? It was better that way.* I sure don't miss that boat. *Although, I would love to acquire a 13 foot Boston Whaler if anyone wants to donate one!*

The key to a good boating day is preparation. The key to a good life is preparation. Some would call preparation, education. Some would call

> Never kick a fresh cow chip on a hot day.
> *Will Rogers*

preparation, financial stability. While others would call preparation, thinking ahead. Jesus gave us some insight when he said, "What kind of builder would build a house without first counting the cost to complete it?" This is why God gave Noah detailed instructions. He did not simply say, "Just build something that floats and sleeps eight adults and a few pets!" For me, preparation can best be defined as a combination of all of the previous definitions, as well as, adding Godly wisdom and Godly direction. Godly wisdom differs from education. One can be brilliant in the ways of this world, but *imbecilic* in God's wisdom. Godly direction is the knowledge of what God wants you to do. Some call it faith.

> I do not feel obliged to believe that the same God who has endowed us with sense, reason and intellect has intended us to forgo their use.
>
> *Galileo Galilei*

As a Christian (Christ-like individual) my goal is to follow the directions of the Creator. He is the One who made me, and it is He who knows how to direct my life in a way that will bring the greatest joy to Him. Reciprocally, when He is happy, I am happy. I often tell my son, "If Daddy aint happy- aint nobody happy!" That is just the way it is. As we delight ourselves in Him, His Word, and His ways; we become fulfilled, completed individuals. This idea is kind of like warning someone not to go on the *It's A Small World* ride at Disney World. You tell them, but they just don't believe, until after the ride, that is. Three years of counseling later, they are still tying to rid their minds of that song. Some of you know what I mean. The mere mention of the song conjures up a memory that will take you all day to forget. Hey, I was trapped in the ride once when it broke down. Two hours of that universalistic- mouse-propaganda melody pounding into my cranium. *Ouch!* I may never be the same. I'm in a twelve-step recovery group even to this day. *"Hi... I'm Mike and I was trapped in It's A Small World for two hours!"*

As you and I delight, consume, and submerge ourselves in the desires of God, He brings real joy and purpose to us. Everything around us says, "If it feels good—do it" The concept of giving one's life over to a Higher Authority, therefore, may sound weird or foreign to us. Nevertheless, it is the right thing to do. Do you want a fulfilled and happy life? Really? *Well... the choice is up to you.* It is only when we combine His wisdom and direction with our frail and willing lives that we experience true fulfillment. Hey let's cut the bull! You have tried to find joy in feeding yourself and it hasn't worked. It hasn't satisfied. When will you wake up and smell reality? If you keep doing the same thing you will get the same results. *Seek your narcissistic quest if you want—but be ready to hold the "L" sign to your wrinkled forehead.*

Delight yourself in the Lord and He will fulfill the real and ultimate desires of your heart. In everything you do acknowledge His leadership and in doing so, your path will be led by Him.
Psalms 37:4-5

I Rode the Short Bus

Friendship is a pretty full-time occupation.

Truman Capote

*L*et me share this with you. It is from an actual ad in the back of a Sky Mall catalog. *"Studies over many decades have proven that a strong command of the English language is directly linked to career advancement, to the money you make, and even to social success. To move ahead in your career, your vocabulary level must at least equal the average level of the members of your profession. To excel, your vocabulary must surpass that of your colleagues. Everyday people judge you by the words you use. Right or wrong, they make assumptions about your intelligence, your education, and your capabilities"* Of course, this was an advertisement designed to sell a vocabulary-building seminar. Never the less, I can't help but wonder how much truth there is to what the ad said. What do you think?

> The only way to have a friend is to be one.
>
> *Ralph Waldo Emerson*

When I was a freshman, I made friends with a senior. His younger brother was my guitar teacher, and the school valedictorian. *Woops, I spelled valedictorian wrong. There I spell-corrected it.* I love computers. I was no valedictorian. I was a "lucky-to-get-to-the-next-class" student. You see, my intelligent friend enjoyed reading the dictionary. *Yes, the dictionary.* While the rest of the guys were reading *Dirt Bike magazines* and *Marvel comic books*, he was learning how to communicate in an educated world. He was no geek…well, maybe he was a bit of a geek, but he was also the star basketball player at our little high school. Maybe that was because he was six-foot, four-inches tall. I'm not really sure. Each day I would approach him in the hall and ask him for a word. He would, obligingly, give me a word. It was always a big two or three syllable word that I could barely pronounce, let alone use in ordinary conversation. Of course, I would try! He would try to explain the word to me, so I could use it correctly. I'm sure I owe him today for some of the words in this book (the bigger ones).

> Often we have no time for our friends but all the time in the world for our enemies.
>
> *Leon Uris*

He had cool, important-sounding words. They were words like colloquialism, consternation, hypo-paretic, carnage, malcontent, endoplasmic, and Polynesian. *Okay, maybe that last word wasn't one of his words but it was all I could think of right now.* I would use them throughout the school day and then at home. I learned that words contained power. I learned that the right words could aptly describe almost any situation. I even began reading the dictionary myself, sometimes just to understand words in the *Dirt Biker* articles. I learned that using some of those words would cause people to stop and listen, sometimes even asking what they meant. Then I could get a little *pride buzz* by explaining it to them, especially if it was an adult who would ask. I could also recognize the people who pretended to know what the words meant, although they had no idea. Kind of like on Wayne's World when Wayne would say, "Sphincter says what" and then someone would say, "What?" Then Wayne and Garth would just laugh and nod. Do you remember that? *Okay, maybe that wasn't the nicest illustration, but, once again, it was all I could think of.* I think my hypo-paretic, iconoclastic tendencies are merging with exploitative cranial impulses again. Woops, there I go again. Truth is, I am a little distracted because I am watching the Dove Awards as I type this. *"Steven Curtis—you go boy!"*

Education can be a great thing, but not if it's merely to feed one's ego. Often a teacher caught me using a big word in the wrong way. They would often feel the need to point it out to me, out loud, in front of the class. I hated that. Still do! *Ouch!* My pride would sting for days! Remember, however, that pride is a big separator. The pride I had in those "big words" caused a barrier between me and other people in my life. I was, at least in my own mind, *BETTER* than they. I knew those words; they didn't! HA! *I was an idiot.* In a world where we really need to come alongside of others, it would do us all a lot of good to remove any barriers we can. As a person who speaks for a living, I can personally attest to that fact. The Apostle Paul penned *that he became all things to all people that he might influence them.* In other words, this highly trained theologian put his theology into the *everyday language* of the person to whom he was talking. I need to do that too. For some, that could mean NOT using *Christianese.* That is a word we use to describe people who talk about God using only big hard-to-understand theological words. For me, it means considering the background of my audience. I must consider who they are and how they communicate.

Be careful not to allow status, position, or even your education to become a stumbling block to your relationships. You may find, as I did, that the pride involved can backfire. In the big world, that kind of pride only leads to humiliation and broken relationships. In other words, people will think you are a jerk and your witness will be nullified. Let's meet people where they are and help them understand what it means to become as a child. A child of the Father. Let's do everything within our power to build bridges to each other instead of motes. Jesus took on the form of a servant! If Jesus can do that… we certainly can. Wow, there's an example for us all. *I hope I wasn't too extemporaneous in my exhortation. Woops I did it again!*

Pride is the first step to a big blunder and a haughty personality is the first step to public disgrace.
Proverbs 16:18

Noah Was a
Drunken Sailor

I hired a general contractor because I didn't need anything specific done.

Mike G. Williams

*D*ennis Miller once said, "This is harder to understand than Bob Dylan reading Finnegan's Wake in a wind tunnel." That is how I feel about Captain Noah and his adventure in faith! If I told the complete truth, I would have to say that I have some real questions about the Noah's Ark adventure. Personally, I don't think Noah brought two of every animal. For example: nexiums terminetrous (Termites). *I have no idea if nexiums terminetrous is a real word but it sounded so scientific.* Think about this for a minute! This is not a "pair of animals" that you really want settling in for a snack on the Lido Deck. I can hear Noah moaning around the bridge while trying to reconcile a damaged hull report with the surprising disappearance of two termites from cage #314.

I have always wondered about the logic involved with the flood. Why destroy the earth with a flood when so many other plagues were so readily available? I mean, hey, you've got your variation on a pestilence theme. Killer frogs are always an option! What about killer boils? Why not combine them? *I can see it now, "Killer Frogs with Boils Attack Mesopotamia this week on Oprah!"* Famine and drought are coming in at a close third behind deadly killer serpents! *But I guess to have serpents that were both deadly and killer would be redundant (and repetitious) (and also overly repetitive).* But seriously, why the flood? Were other ways just too slow? Maybe the Creator didn't have time to wait around that year so…crack…lightning…thunder! Forty days later it was all over. This took much longer than forty days when you really look at the calendar. Check it out. Time did not seem to be a problem for God. He gave Noah one-hundred and twenty years to build the Ark in the first place! *And you thought your contractor was slow.*

Another thing that is hard for me to understand is that, after hearing personally from God, building the S.S. Faith Boat, seeing God deliver him and his family, and being given the world as his backyard, Noah still got depressed. Then before you know it, pop-fizz, Noah is drunk off his rocker. *I actually don't know if they had rockers at that point in history. This is mere speculation.* I am not even going to follow this story any farther, but the outcome wasn't good. How does a guy who has heard so profoundly from God, lose sight of the great vision? Here is a dude who built the ark in the middle of the residential district, fought zoning restrictions, building inspectors, and thieving sub-contractors. He had to deal with unscrupulous animal dealers trying to sell him three legged leopards and horses painted to look like zebra's. He faced ridicule from everyone around him for years, yet still remained faithful to the plan. Now he sees the big plan come true before his eyes, and what does he do? He gets drunk and takes his clothes off. I might suggest that it was post-traumatic distress syndrome from hearing, "Are we there yet?" a hundred times a day… from each kid…for the entire rainy season. *Who wouldn't snap like a Louie Anderson suspender strap?*

> There are two things that they talk about in the Bible; wine and stuff that is really hard to believe… unless you have been sampling the wine.
>
> *Blaine Adams*

Is it any different today? How do those who have known the truth, seen the truth, experienced the truth, lived the truth, and walked the truth, suddenly walk away from it? Did they really believe the truth in the first place, or was it all just a game? It scares me to think that I could somehow declare war on the same faith that I have grown trust. This scenario scares the *mookie* out of me. It scares me to my knees.

Why does God pick these losers? Does He not look into the future with these prophetic candidates? Does he really limit his own foreknowledge like that? I need to give some managerial advice here to the heavenly kingdom. Look ahead! You have got the technology. You have got the authority. You have got the tools. Use them. Assign an angel to find a long-term guy. Surely, there must be somebody. *I could give you a few names!*

Sometimes I think God chooses to specially bless future failures. *But why?* Biblical history records many of them. Some are even listed as His favorites. *But why?* That makes no sense to me; however, it does however encourage me to be a little more forgiving and a little less condemning of the *fallen* individual as I try to stand against evil myself. *I could become just as easily entangled!* I often remind myself that the righteousness of my life will one day be revealed too. I'm sure that some of my activities with which I took great spiritual pride; things I thought were so right, will turn out to be so very wrong.

Today, let us plead for the grace and mercy to stand against temptation, and the stamina to live for Him for the duration of our days here on this globe. Let us be a little less condemning of those who have fallen victim to the deceiver, and let us be willing to forgive them, as God through Christ has forgiven us. *Yeah, and be careful with the Boones Farm!*

> The church, by and large, has had a poor record of encouraging freedom. She has spent so much time inculcating in us the fear of making mistakes, that she has made us like ill-taught piano students: we play our songs, but we never really hear them because our main concern is not to make music but to avoid some flub.
>
> *Robert Capon*

Do not be overly sure of yourself, pay careful attention or you could fall too.
1 Corinthians 10:12

105

It's All About Me

I know there are people in this world who do not love their fellow man, and I hate people like that!

Tom Lehrer

I am invisible in some Restaurants. *Yes, invisible!* Even at 270 pounds, I walk in, stand there, stand there, stand there, and wait, and wait, clear my throat, clear my throat again, and then, maybe, I get a hostess to look me in the eye. Do I look like a bad tipper? Did I forget to use my deodorant? *Maybe they are afraid I might just clear the buffet before closing time.* Maybe I should wear a nicer brand of clothing? Something that says, "I'm a nice guy and a good tipper!" Has this ever happened to you?

Last week my wife reminded me of a book she had read by John Ortberg. In it he proposed that 80% of what we do, we do to make an impression on others. I personally would like to think that I haven't reached that level of pride, but, hmmm, maybe 65%. *But, at least I'm humble about it!* I wonder how much of what I really do, I do to make people see me in a certain way. You know, the way I want them to perceive me. I own a copy of Dress for Success, which I have not read, but the title keeps me thinking classy. Sometimes I wonder how much of my life is spent trying to convince people I am "All that—and a bucket of

> To my way of thinking, neighbors are like hair plugs: The less you notice them, the better they are.
>
> *Dennis Miller*

chicken!" Seriously! Hey, I'm still amazed that a little name-dropping will get me a good table at the Shogun. Is that wrong? C'mon', is it? *It is one thing to grovel, but it is entirely another thing to create a perception whereby the best deal can be accrued through pseudo-personal relationship strategies or artificial identities.*

This morning we were introduced to a new song at church. The projector illuminated the text and I began to sing, "It's all about You Jesus, and all this is for You, for Your glory and Your praise, it's not about me..." I was singing away in my "sit next to me and be blessed by my award winning voice" until I realized what I was really singing. *OUCH!* It's hard for me to sing that song with gusto because *the truth* is quite often the complete opposite of those words! Those are strong-tough words to sing with integrity in a world seemingly designed to accentuate the opposite. I so desire to be thought "well of" that I even hit the spell check every couple of minutes so that anyone who walks in the room will not see how badly I spell from the *little red lines* all over the page. It's all about Jesus... yeah, sure. *Should I wear boots when I sing that song?*

> I rented a Geo Metro last week, which is the only car that allows you to sit in the driver's seat and touch every window in the car. I felt like Fred Flintstone every time I came to a stop. My feet still hurt.
>
> *Taylor Mason*

Wow! It's tough to make it *ALL* about Jesus. Even for a minister! I once stood behind a pulpit engraved with the words, "We want to see Jesus". I said to myself, "Me too... good luck!" *I delivered an extremely short sermon that day.* For the same reason you *can't* sell a Lexus and a Geo Metro at the same time, I have come to believe that it is nearly impossible to show people how great I am (hypothetically speaking of course) and how good God is, at the same time. Some things *cannot* be done simultaneously.

It comes back to that evil twin called PRIDE. It creeps up on us as little children and hides in the dark shadows of our cranium. It is the filter that keeps our witness to a minimum, while simultaneously keeping our hair flawless. It keeps our attitude one of superiority, and squelches words of honest praise for others around us. It slips into our workdays though one-ups-manship around the drinking fountain or in the break room. It convinces us to purchase houses and new vehicles that we can't afford so we can be viewed as successful. It is a lover of credit cards, for it always spends more than it can afford, and *by nature* promises much more than it can actually deliver. *All of this for the sheer rush of impression.*

Wouldn't it be wonderful if I could find the *gene of pride* and have it surgically removed? *I would be so proud of myself for doing that!* Only the exposure of my heart, to the light and perfection of Jesus and His Word, can pride really be burned from the core of my life. Only then can I honestly sing, "It's all about You Jesus…" My pride, however, stubbornly refuses to let go. Its hungry tentacles must by pried off, one self concern at a time. And that hurts. As it happens, my singing softens and those words "About you, Jesus" are becoming a daily prayer of desire. "I want it to be all about Jesus" How is it with you? Are you invisible yet?

> Don't be so humble.
> You're not that great.
> *Golda Meier*

When pride enters a life it is followed quickly by shame, but with the humble abides wisdom.
Proverbs 11:2

Shakespeare Is My Destiny

Some people see things that are, and ask why? Some people dream of things that never were, and ask why not? Some people have to go to work and don't have time for all that.

George Carlin

*A*fter *Turkey Soup for the Sarcastic Soul volume #2* was released, people asked me why I wrote a second book. I usually blurted out, "I needed the money! I plan on using the money to take some writing classes at the local junior college or maybe buy a Jeep." *I always wanted to own a Jeep.* The truth is I bought a Jeep with money from the first book. My wife thinks I wrote another book because I don't want to be another Francis Scot Key, which is true as well. I mean, how many times have you heard people say, "Sure he wrote the Star Spangled Banner... but what else?" *Another one hit wonder goes down on the field of VH-1's, Where Are They Now.* With only one song to your credit, you don't even get your own half hour History Channel Special. You wind up a bubble in some Pop-Up Video.

> My Agent would tell you that my books are #1 Best Sellers! That true! They were the #1 Best Sellers at every family reunion I ever attended.
> *Mike G. Williams*

A few years ago, Paula Cole penned and performed a song that contained the phrase, *I don't want to wait for my life to be over, I want to know right now how will it be.* It was one of those songs that radio stations wore slap out for two years. Before it ran its course we were all singing, "I don't want to wait for this song to be over!" Nevertheless, at least the quoted tag line speaks volumes to me. I want my life to be worthy of the oxygen it cost the planet. I want to be participating in the miraculous, the immortal, the eternal, and the supernatural. A man of destiny, surrounded by people of destiny, and attending a church of destiny! Can you hear the Superman theme music playing in the background as you read these words? I can't either. But it was a nice thought.

Destiny is a contemporary power word that is thrown around quite frequently. The word itself seems to promote the idea of world renown or even iconic. Say the word out loud. "Destiny!" It has a strong, royal ring to it, don't you think? Are we to be a people of destiny? I think so, but maybe not in the way modern culture implies. The dictionary states that *des-ti-ny* means "something that *[is to]* happen to a particular person or thing or a *predetermined* course of events." Hmmm? I really want my life to count for something. I desire to make some sort of gigantic splash in this human gene pool. Think for a moment. What if my predetermined course of events was, merely, to quietly raise my children in the nurture and admonition of the Lord? What if my predetermined course could be to love God, love my neighbor, and never write another book? Am I going to be okay with that? *It's a legitimate question.*

> It took me fifteen years to discover I had no talent for writing, but I couldn't give it up because by that time I was too famous.
>
> *Robert Benchley*

I have quoted William McNamara many times, and I will again. McNamara said, "I stake the future on the few humble and hearty lovers who seek God passionately in the marvelous, messy world of redeemed and related realities that lie in front of our noses." I need to remember that the marvelous, messy world of redeemed is not always full of glitter and headlines. The messy world often operates without the aid of lights or electricity. More often, that *messy* world is lived and carried out in quiet ambiguity. I might describe it as, "behind the scenes."

I fully believe my destiny is, that I be conformed to the image of Jesus Christ, to close my eyes at the end of the day and rest contentedly in His hands. That may include forty years of anonymity or even a cross. That may include self-sacrifice, prayer, and working with some undesirable disciples. The road I travel may not take me more than a few miles from my childhood home or birthplace. I may never have my name on a business card or billboard. I may never have a six-figure income, or even a five-figure income, for that matter. I might see many great miracles, or I may be unappreciated because I am simply another hometown boy. Regardless of the visibility of the path, the Creator God has declared my destiny, and I will not turn back. I don't have to wait for my life to be over. I will join God in His glorious destiny of *conformation to Him*, and rest assured that my life is counting on His grand scale.

> No race can prosper until it learns there is as much dignity in tilling a field as there is in writing a poem.
>
> *Booker T. Washington*

So my friend, don't consider your present position in this life to be trivial. Live your life to the fullest. Suck from the moisture of each day as if it were your last drop of water. Give each day all that you have. Make today your best day ever, and if God gives you another day or another week, give that one your best too. Make your choice to be like Jesus… who being in the form of God… and unlike us—truly equal with God… made himself of "no reputation" and became a servant unto death for our redemption.

God has already chosen for you a glorious destiny; that you should be conformed to the likeness of His Son.
Romans 8:29

Woops I Did It Again

We've got drive-by shootings now... How lazy do you have to be, to be too lazy to get out of the car to shoot someone? It's a sorry world.

Mike G. Williams

*N*ow you may not believe this, but I can be a bit sarcastic at times. As I have mentioned in past books, it is my only spiritual gift. I have not found any Biblical references for the *gift of sarcasm* yet, but mark my words, when they finish the reconstruction of the Dead Sea Scrolls, the truth will be known. *I fully expect to see Solomon's Book of Sarcasm or maybe Paul's letter to the Comedians at Thessalonica.* And of course I mean "sarcasm" in the nicest and most humorous of terms. I firmly believe that Paul had this gift as well, so I'm in good company. This gift often leads me to comment, out loud, on things that I don't understand. I especially like it when people go around spouting biblical-ish or Christian-ese type phrases. Is there any more fodder for a sarcastic soul than that? I doubt it! *So rock-on you bastions of baboonery!*

I have a hard time listening to those five-thousand-watt religious radio stations! You know the ones, right? Of course banjo and organ are the Biblical instruments of choice. The shows are always hosted by a back-woods preacher with an accent torn from the script of *Sling Blade*. He proclaims, "If'n the good Low-rd didn't want you to eat pigs... He wouldn't have made them out of meat!" *Yeah, and if the good Lord didn't want us to smoke pot he wouldn't have made the leaves flammable! Follow that thinking—duh!* You can hear some mighty fine heresy and some mighty fine stupidity spouted in the name of all that is supposed to be Holy. *It's not just heretical remarks that bother me... okay...maybe it is... I do like banjos.*

I struggle not to be sarcastic with the people who blurt out religious phrases like they are bumper stickers on the back of a rusty 1978 Pinto Wagon. If you're going to blurt out a tidbit of wisdom, at least have the common courtesy to stop and explain exactly what you mean. Stop the spiritual "drive-bys" and get out of your car. Explain yourself... *If* you can.

Maybe that is why people shout their opinions; that way they don't require explanation. "Wait on the Lord. That's what you need to do, Mike!" *Thanks for that wisdom Sister Know It All! But...what does it mean to wait...and for how long?* What if I ignore what God has already told me what to do? Should I

> Most of the people I see "waiting on the Lord" are just lazy!
>
> *Tim DeTellis*

wait for Him to give me another option or maybe change His mind? What does it mean to "wait" on the Lord? I have learned that there is a huge difference between waiting on the Lord and sitting lazily on your tail!

Let me chase this *waiting* rabbit for a moment. Most of us "wait" in a horizontal position, lying on our back, sleeping. Waiting on God is supposed to be more like doing the work of a great waiter or waitress at a great restaurant. You stand ready for the customer's special request. While you are waiting, however, you continue to serve what you know the customer wants. You continue to fill his water glass. You continue to clean his plates. You continue to pour the wine (if your customer is not Baptist). You make sure that the tablecloth is clean and the silverware shiny. Eventually, the customer says, "I need you to go and get me a flask of A-1 Sauce." Then you hop to it! It can be a long dinner before the customer ever asks for you to retrieve the A-1 Sauce. It may be quite a few moments before he wants you to fetch the dessert menu. Your job, however, is to *serve faithfully* while you *wait.* You do what you know to do as you wait patiently for the special commands. I once had a waiter call the restaurant next door trying to find the type of salad dressing I had requested. Needless to say, the tip showed my appreciation. Wouldn't it be fair to believe that God's tip will too?

I remember being at Pepperdine University! I felt as if I had "arrived" as a speaker. To be asked to do one of the four yearly chapel services was quite an honor. They probably would not have a chapel at all were it not for the yearly one hundred thousand dollar endowment with the words "mandatory chapel" emblazoned upon it. Some of you are doing the math… no; I did not get one-fourth of that. *The school is not holding these "highly controversial" chapels to break-even financially.* As a very secular school, they have to offer chapel attendance as a credited elective to get any of the student body to attend. They told me not to expect much of a response from anyone other than the very small handful of Christian kids. I was told that most students would simply sit there and do their homework, or read the paper, while others might be a bit more vocally antagonistic. *Hecklers…at a chapel service? I could get into that!* Much to my surprise, the event went wonderfully, and the students sat attentively as I sweated through every word. *For that I give a special thanks to my Ken Davis Dynamic Communicator Workshop video courses!*

> Man does not live by words alone, despite the fact that sometimes he has to eat them.
> *Adlai E. Stevenson*

After that wonderful chapel service, I stood at the back of the hall greeting students and signing CD's. On each CD I signed my name in a sweeping artistic form and jotted the reference Psalms 37:7. Many students where befuddled that a person could perform comedy without being dirty or using profanity. One girl said, "I never heard a comedian be funny without saying the *F* word." I guess in some places, "dirty and profane" is just the expected norm. I thanked them all and humbly explained that I believed you didn't have to be dirty to be funny.

A few days later, I began to receive some strange e-mail. Their correspondences suggested that I had been rude and crass in my verse selection. I had no idea what I had written that could have upset anyone. I questioned those who had e-mailed me, and soon found out. Apparently, I had written Psalm 38:7 instead of Psalm 37:7. *I wish I could tell you that I instantly knew what that verse said, but I didn't.* Upon closer inspection of my trusty KJV desktop Bible, I found the problem. What should have said, "Rest in the Lord and wait patiently for Him (Psalms 37:7)," now said, "In my loins there is a loathsome disease (Psalms 38:7)." Needless to say, I was very embarrassed and sent many proper apologies. The "Mr. Clean" Comedy Guy has just been crass without knowing it… sorry. *Sometimes I think about putting that verse on a bumper sticker as a witnessing tool! It needs less explanation than most of the bumper stickers I see.*

Anyone can make a mistake. Some mistakes are bigger than others, but I sincerely desire to let my words be carefully chosen so that those words edify our great Savior and advance the kingdom of God. Choose your words carefully today. There may be some words that you want to remove from your personal vocabulary, or a phrase or two from your mental thesaurus. We may never have the opportunity to get deeply involved in someone else's life. Most people will only know us by our words, phrases, and the demeanor in which we deliver them.

> We've got to pause and ask ourselves: How much clean air do we need?
>
> *Lee Iacocca*

Back to our subject! Wait on the Lord. Serve Him, and as you serve Him, listen for what He especially requires of you. Waiting on your back only leads to laziness! You certainly don't want to be asleep when the Master needs you to run next door and get Him some A-1 Sauce! How are you waiting on Him today?

Rest in the Lord and
wait patiently for Him.
Psalms 37:7

(And while you are waiting...
be careful what references you use)

Lunch-lady Land

If stupidity got us into this mess, then why can't it get us out?

Will Rogers

*T*here is a point at which food service people take their sanitation formula too seriously. I had just finished setting up my act under a tent in the ninety-five degree heat. "Run over and grab a dinner from the picnic area before you do your show," my host said. So…I headed over to the uncovered trays of chicken, green beans, coleslaw, and brownies that were being kept fresh by the blazing sun and swarming flies. I reach down and grasped a piece if chicken with the stainless steel tongs and pulled it toward my plate. "Put the chicken down sir," I heard coming from my immediate vicinity. A tall girl of about eighteen years of age emerged from the shadows resembling *Seinfeld's Soup Nazi* with the addition of a tongue piercing and a hair net.

"Ma'am, what's the problem? Has it gone bad?" I shyly said.

To that she retorted, "You can't handle food without gloves."

"I appreciate the thought ma'am," I spattered back, "but I intend to eat the food without gloves on because I just don't care for that oily plastic-glove taste. And for the record, I am not handling the food; I am handling the tongs!"

At this point she reaches into the aluminum tray, eschews the flies from the poultry and puts a piece on my plate.

"Ma'am, I was kind of hoping I could have the chicken leg that I already violated with my unsanitary [who knows what germ they are carrying] hands."

"Sir," she said snidely, "This is not a restaurant where you get to pick and choose what you get."

Now this was where I lost my cool. "Let me get this straight, Lady... I can't touch my own food with tongs, but you can touch everything out here and then grab my chicken with your plastic, ecolli-ish virus-transferring, hand-covering device! I can go over to the fruit and run my hands through the self-service fruit bowl, all the while sneezing and coughing on the fruit that is going to be immediately consumed by unsuspecting guests, but I can't pick up my own heated chicken leg with a set of tongs! Hmmm." She tried to interrupt, but I didn't let her. "Be quiet Ma'am, I'm still venting! I can go over to those big coolers and drink from the tap if I want to, or return my spittle-rimed glass back to the said-same self-service dispenser spout as many times as I want, but I can't touch my own lunch!! Ma'am, how do you people here in *Lunch Lady Land* eat? Should I have one of your fishnet-headed friends hold it for me while I eat it? Well, that is, eat the piece you want me to eat because I can't be allowed to pick out my own chicken leg, even though I am the last person in the line and by law (I really wasn't sure about this) the rest of this *swill* has to be thrown away. Do I have this straight?"

> I saw this water safety manual that actually says if a shark attacks, you should poke it in the eyes! Who wrote that, the Three Stooges?
>
> *Larry Reeb*

She slipped in a short, "Sir, it is for your own good."

This gave me time to inhale and continue, "So is running over there and yanking that cigarette out of that man's mouth so I won't have to experience second-hand smoke! So is burying your car to cut down on carbon dioxide emissions! So is having a test to see who should procreate! Which could have annulled our discussion if a procreation test had been in existence eighteen years and nine months ago (this eighteen year old girl didn't understand that statement at all—overly mathematical I guess). Ma'am, I'm not trying to be sarcastic here (a small lie), but you need more than plastic gloves to validate sanitation. Just try and be understanding to a stranger who does not understand the Ohio food standard act of '74'. Now I'm going to walk over there and put this piece of chicken on the grill for a minute to warm it up a bit, burn off the fly residue, make it a little safer, aye?"

She had the audacity to respond by saying, "Sir, you can't go near the grill; it is a safety hazard."

> As yet there have been no deaths attributed to killer bees. However, two bees were caught this week planning a murder.
> *Dennis Miller*

I may have been entirely wrong in my response to that young lady. *Okay, let me say there was no excuse for my verbal outburst (although my medications had not kicked in at that time).* Truth being told, I really appreciate a clean restaurant, and I applaud an honest, contemplative effort also. I wish we would all take as much concern for what we put in our bodies as we do for the type of oil we put in our cars. I believe, however, that we have once again been fooled into worrying about the things that don't matter, while we overlook the things that do. Jesus dealt with this when he said the Pharisees paid a tithe on every new leaf in their garden, but they overlooked the weightier matters of God's law. He applauded their tithing, but reprimanded their forgetting the other aspects of the Law. Maybe he was talking about that "love your neighbor" part? Hmmm!

Which aspect of the Law have you placed all your idealism and support behind? We all have our pet principles. Our soapboxes! Our favorite Laws! Which ones would you prefer that I did not mention right now? *For me it might be gluttony!* Would you admit we often overlook the weightier matters of the Law? *Love*...now *THAT* is a weighty law! Do we distribute those "Laws of God" in a loving and grace-filled way? Or do we spout forth the "Laws of God" in sanctimonious self-righteous authority? How we share, really makes a difference. You know it does. We both know it does. *And I certainly didn't share my viewpoint (although correct) in a posture of love.*

As we go to work today, we need to act and react in love. Be sensitive to those who are not familiar with the Food Service Act of 74 and show a little mercy. Just maybe, I should show a little mercy to those who make their living upholding the Food Service Act. My wife has been known to say to me, "Thank you for being so kind as to look beyond the large log in your own eye to help me get the speck of dust out of mine!" And I am willing to look beyond my own visual log jam to help others with their "speck" problem! It's just the way I am. My calling! My cross to bear! I'm more than a giver; my Doctor says that I am a "carrier!" How would this apply to you this week?

Allow brotherly love to flourish among you each and every day.
Hebrew 13:1

Why Did the Turtle Cross The Road?

When a man won't listen to his conscience, it is usually because he doesn't want advice from a total stranger.

unknown

J like to consider myself something of a humanitarian, especially when it comes to animals. I guess that would make me a *Anama-tarian*, if there is such a thing. When I was a kid I dragged home every sick bird and mangy cat I found along that long road. I even wanted to be a veterinarian, until I found out that it required eight years of college. *So…I just settled on comedian, which only required taking a few night classes at a Jr. College, passing a driver's test, and watching a lot of television.* Yet, even today I will stop along the road to help an animal if I possibly can. If you read *Turkey Soup Volume One*, you know that those animals have ranged from cows to alligators. I even helped a six-foot-long rattlesnake one time. I have pictures to prove that one! Helping an occasional wounded bird or turtle, therefore, is all part of my Florida lifestyle.

I guess the most interesting part of helping a wild animal is that they never actually realize that they are being helped. There have been times when I wanted to say to the little critter, "Either you be nice to me or I will make sure you are the hood ornament on the next passing semi!" Turtles are the poster-children for ungrateful roadside assistance. First off, they cross the road as if they own it. *"Hey I'm green, and I got a shell, and I'm coming across…"* I can't help but wonder why they even need to get to the land across the road anyway. Was the five hundred acres on their current

side of the road just too small for them? Do they suffer from the same con-
quest tendencies that we do? Is there a problem with turtle overcrowding?
Maybe there is an insect shortage? Do they know something we don't
know? I think it is just a turtle's nature to roam. Roam slowly, but roam.
It's not like they have other things to do. There are no turtle movie theatres
or even turtle restaurants, well, none that I know of. In the south, they
might be the bill of fare in a few restaurants! And outside of the Teenage
Mutant Ninja Turtles there are very few turtle stars. In fact, I doubt that the real turtles know that Ninja Turtles even exist. *It must be tough growing up without a hero!*

> Wisdom is the ability
> to correctly apply
> knowledge.
> *Terica L. Williams*

The last time I went to Channel 22 WCLF TV in Clearwater, I passed my host, Herman Bailey, on the side of the road trying to help a turtle. There was Herman, perfect hair, perfect teeth, perfectly dressed, stooping in the sweltering heat, trying to rescue a mossy green snapper from the spinning Firestone wheels of death. I don't understand the turtle's mindset. Herman is obviously not a hungry redneck! *This is someone who looks gentler than Mr. Rogers on Ritalin.* Yet, the turtle is trying with all his might to stretch its head back far enough to bite the hand trying to protect it. Dumb turtle! Can't they see this guy is giving them life? I guess not.

Well Herman escaped with his fingers in tact. Barely! Fortunately! Fingers are important for a man who works in television. *There is something amazingly distracting about a guy waving his hands in front of a hundred thousand people with his fingertip dangling from a knuckle.* I think it would take your mind off of the real subject of the show! *"Thousands of people are starving—yeah whatever—look at that dude's fingers—freeky!"* Nevertheless, with the help of Herman, the turtle got to safety, and the other road travelers were protected from a possible collision with one of these ancient creatures.

The greatest lesson in this story is one of the reasons I stop for turtles. It is probably the reason Herman does too. It is the lesson of *The Turtle On the Gatepost.* Do you remember that old saying? "When you see a turtle on top of a gatepost, you know he didn't get there by himself." Yeah, now you remember it. Comparison: I am the turtle; God is the Herman Bailey. Most of the time, I fight help, assistance, wisdom, experience, and insight; and I fight them with a vengeance. I often want to bite the very hand that feeds me, if I could. Then in a moment, in the twinkling of an eye, I find myself in a better place, a safer position, because of the help of another. Wow!

Why do we fight the leading of God? Why do we constantly strive to find a bigger or better pasture? Isn't it time we stopped fighting the One who sees beyond this high grass that we are wading through? Isn't it time we quit trying to out think the One who sees beyond bend in the road and sees the approaching semi truck? Let's also remember that we have only achieved as much as we have through His grace and mercy. It, therefore, makes sense to let Him lift me up to the top of the fence if He chooses. It is a place that is impossible for me to go without Him. *Try as I may—still impossible!*

Trust in the Lord with all your heart and mind, and don't rely on your own ability to understand His ways. Our understanding is often weak and shallow. Salute His Lordship daily and He will direct your paths. Run from evil and it shall be as health to you.
Proverbs 3:5-8

I Should Have
Worn My Pants

In three words I can sum up everything I know about life: it goes on.

Robert Frost

*T*oday, I went back to the Alfred P. Murrah Federal Building in Oklahoma City. Well, actually, to where it once stood. It has been many years since that fateful day of April 19, 1995. Much has happened since that inhumane April morning. Today I sit in a beautiful commemorative park where the Federal Building once stood. To be quite honest with you, I thought my return visit would spur thoughts of our nation being systematically corrupted by a decay of our moral infrastructure. *I could write for hours on that topic* But, that was not on my mind.

Rather, I was moved to tears as I walked a section of chain-link fence. This fence had become a makeshift memorial wall, where wire ties and scotch tape hold fast the pictures of loved ones senselessly slaughtered that day. The pictures of children jolted me the most. Perhaps it is because I am a father. I am a father who could not begin to understand the loss of a child. My pace slowed as I read each card and every poem written by those left behind. After a few minutes of weeping behind my dark sunglasses, a site that is not foreign to the many visitors that come there every year to pay their respects, I came across a letter written by the wife of a victim. This was a letter of thanks for many years of happy marriage. There were words of recollection and memories. There were words involving their children. This weather-beaten letter spoke volumes about the character of the departed. The letter closed with a thank you to this husband for leaving his wife with a verse of scripture. I have no idea the circumstances in which he shared this scripture throughout his life. She simply wrote, Thank you for giving me the scripture: I know the plans I have for you, plans for good, for you to prosper and have life... (Jeremiah 29:11).

In light of the situation and surroundings, this verse almost seemed like a slap in the face to a faith that we somehow blindly trust. But nevertheless, the scripture still stands untouched by the blast of fertilizer and kerosene from a Ryder rental truck. I struggle with a God who knows the plans He has for me which may very well include tragedy. *I've quoted Max Lucado before, and I will quote him again. He said, "Opportunity knocks but tragedy kicks the door in."*

This Memorial Park now stands where an office once stood, an aesthetically beautiful reminder of man's ruthlessness and injustice. There are 168 memorial chairs representing those who lost their lives that morning. Next to the chairs is a tranquil pool of water, and beside that pool is an elm tree. Though tattered and burned, the old tree was one of the few survivors of the blast. Cars, windows, buildings, and other trees in an eight-block radius were scarred and destroyed; yet this old twenty-foot-tall elm tree stood the blast rooted deeply in the Oklahoma soil. *How quietly profound.* A tree deeply rooted in the soil survived the blast. Hmmm.

> Injustice anywhere is injustice everywhere.
> *Martin Luther King*

This is a book of illustrations, parallels, and comparisons, but trying to make sense of a tragedy like this is far beyond my ability. I cannot make a parallel that says all of those who were deeply rooted became the survivors; I wish I could, but unfortunately some did not. I do appreciate, however, the fact that at least one made it. One tree becomes a tribute to life. *A tribute to the fact that life goes on.* A battered tree becomes a seed of hope for future generations. A battered tree will once again spread its branches, bare its seed, and the wind will carry that seed to every corner of the nation.

As I stood there with tear-moistened sunglasses, the words of a song sprang forth like an unexpected spring shower. They do so often when our emotions meet the unexplainable. I believe Bill and Gloria Gaither penned my little unexpected treasure so many years ago. I can still hear Bill singing, *"When you've knelt beside the rubble of an aching broken heart, when the things you gave your life to have fallen apart, your not the first to be acquainted with sorrow, grief, or pain, but the Master promised to bring sunshine after the rain, Hold on my child, joy comes in the morning, your weeping only lasts through the night…"* Wow, another phenomenally contemporary way of resounding, *I know the plans I have for you says the Lord.*

For me, the hardest part of the Christian faith is calling God good in the midst of things we do not understand. I say that from absolute, heartfelt experience. I have been asked to realize that He has plans for me, even though I may not understand them at times. I must attempt to take comfort in the knowledge that He is good! *He may not be safe… but He is good.* And tomorrow we will be able to stand with our heads held high, although the tears still sting our eyes and say that He has turned our mourning into dancing.

The cabby, who shuttled me around on my visit, was on duty that fateful and historical April morning. He told me many stories through his own tears, and as he motored me out to the airport, he told me about a man who was staying at the YMCA across the street from the Federal Building. The man was blown out of bed by the explosion. His clothes were in the closet when the blast hit and were sucked into the collapsing wall. Blown from his bed by this rude awakening, he realized that he had to immediately evacuate the building. With his clothes gone, he wrapped his pillowcase around his body and felt his way along the staircase of the old building. Now wearing nothing but a Sesame Street pillowcase with an Elmo face emblazoned on the front of it, he ran down the stairs and out the door. Standing in the midst of hundreds of people who had raced to the scene, he realized he's wearing a Sesame Street Elmo pillowcase for trousers. My cabby got the guy into his cab and whisked him to a shelter. *In the midst of all this terror the young man looked at the cabby and said, "I guess I should have grabbed the Big Bird blanket instead."* The cabby and I laughed. I now have a better understanding of George Bernard Shaw's remark. He unashamedly said, "Life does not cease to be funny when people die; any more than it ceases to be serious when people laugh." Yes I know I have said that before too, but hey, that's deep, and it bears repeating. One day I hope to fully believe it.

Sometimes the situations of life are rather unexplainable. There are things I can find purpose in if I look hard enough, but unfortunately many things I cannot. I couldn't find purpose in some things with all the

> A god who let us prove his existence would be an idol.
>
> *Dietrich Bonhoeffer*

searching in the world. If you're honest, neither can you. *So I wait.* I place them on my unexplained list. I put them at the top of my question list, and I will ask them someday. But for now, I place my trust in God and find my faith bound up in the most famous *God ordained* tragedy of all. Yes, the cross. Maybe it wasn't such a tragedy after all.

> Life does not cease to be funny when people die, any more than it ceases to be serious when people laugh.
> *George Bernard Shaw*

What can wash away my sins? Nothing but the blood of Jesus! Precious is the gift that brought life, and health, and peace to my soul. Precious becomes that great tragedy, though I still don't fully understand it.

I know the plans I have for you, plans for peace, plans for you to prosper and have life.
Jeremiah 29:11

Death to Olin Mills

The sign said fine for littering, so I threw my trash out the window!

Justin Fennell

J'm getting ready to get some new headshots. Headshots are those pictures that speakers and entertainers use for promotional material. Heavily airbrushed facial photo's that make us appear to be interesting, humorous, important, lenitive, and knowledgeable. *Just to name a few.* For the many of you who have never seen me before you purchased this book, let me simply say that I never won Mr. Photogenic in high school. *The twenty-plus years of passage since that time has not seemed to aid the situation either.* You will never see the little un-retouched caption under my ugly mug. "Send in a team of airbrush artist's and let them go to work. *Overtime!* Call Eastman Kodak if need be!" I have actually considered using a stunt double for photo shoots; however, anyone who remotely resembles me, probably shouldn't be photographed either. *I once had my colors done at Burdine's, and the girl said that I was a "Nuclear Winter." I'm not certain, but I think that is pretty bad.*

My secretary, Phyllis, suggested that I get a little color on my face before the next photo shoot. Like many others living in Florida, I just don't get the chance to get out in the sun. *There is such a short season!* She suggested that I order some of the Home Shopping Network's Instant Tanning Solution to give me a little color. Well, the problem is, I remember my mom getting some of this stuff thirty years ago. It streaked so badly she looked like an orange and white zebra. In my case, that could be an improvement; however, I respectfully rejected the idea of ordering the tan in a can. She assured me that Home Shopping Network had been offering this new stuff that really works. No streaks! No yellowing! No blotches! So… with great hesitation and reluctance I told her to order some for me.

Two days later I'm looking at a thirty-nine dollar bill for two little one-ounce jars of peanut butter colored ointment. One marked Quickie-tan and the other simply marked Exfoliator. The word exfoliator sounds like an Arnold Swartzinager film. *"I am the Exfoliator… I'll be back… I'll clean your dead skin… and your pores… and run for governor… you veee-ka-ling!"* But before you could say, "tan line," I was in the bathtub, exfoliating my skin to a pre-tanning condition. Then I carefully began applying the tanning sauce. It worked pretty well despite the fact that it smelled like embalming fluid. For the

> I'm so glad that messy hair came in fashion. If we can get that goop in your eye, and bad breath to come in style, I'd be ready before I wake up.
>
> *Matt Jernigan*

next twenty-four hours I had a beautiful autumn glow. Yet despite my best efforts, the photos turned out like they always do. I looked like the home-coming queen at the All-Gothic High School Prom. *Well, except for the fact that I smiled and I haven't pierced every square inch of my cranium!*

I did get one good laugh out of the matter. As I read the label on the back of the little tanning solution bottle, along with the directions and a few "approved by" stamps, there was a one-line statement. It jumped out at me in bold letters. It said, "NOT TESTED ON ANIMALS." Did I need to know this? I never heard a grandma say, "My little foo-foo has been looking so pale, but the sun just dries out her wee little skin. If she could just get a good tan…." Seriously people, why not test the stuff on animals? The PETA people (People for the Ethical Treatment of Animals) are always telling us "animals are people too." *Then, dog gone it (sorry for the pun), they deserve a tanning alternative too.* Why are we not testing this stuff on lab rats? You say, "Oh that would be cruel." Oh yes, the stuff just might permanently tan that rat. The other rats might reject him as a fellow member of the rodent family, and he would feel depressed and ostracized. Tell me, who or what do they test this stuff on? Do they go down to the orphanage and get a few dozen unsuspecting children? *That would be so much more humane? "Yes Sir Doctor Franken-tan."* On a personal note, I don't give a *rat's tanned behind,* if they test the stuff on animals. I think we need to know if we could use it on our dog, cat, ferret, cockatiel, or goldfish for that matter. *I DEMAND EQUAL RIGHTS FOR SQUIRRELS!* I'm, therefore, urging you to call your congressman today and stop animal, product-use discrimination. *Foo-foo deserves a tanning alternative!*

The point with the tan stuff, is basically to appear as if we have a tan, when we really do not. Wow, don't we spend a lot of time and money trying on appearances? We have this great fixation on looking good, *QUICK!* Give us a product that requires no time or effort, yet looks as if it did. From tanning and diets, to microwaves ovens and minute rice, we are obsessed with speed and ease! *I'm waiting to see 30 Second Rice, for the days when Minute Rice is just too time consuming.* Most of the quick fixes in life have left me desiring something else, like a slowly cooked non-micro-insta-waved dinner made from fresh vegetables and homemade everything! Even our theology has fallen victim to an instantaneous mentality.

> I'm waiting to see 30 Second Rice, for the days when Minute Rice is just too time consuming.
>
> *Mike G. Williams*

I believe that the quick fix theology is why we seek counsel other places, rather than scripture. Sometimes the Law of God can seem somewhat brutal. The admonitions of scripture often require a more holy-istic (my own word!) approach to life than I care to participate in. The teachings of Christ constantly call us to repentance, self-discipline, self-denial, and long-term accountability. The Great Commission itself seems to suggest that the Christian Faith be tempered with the understanding that it is a discipleship process. The word discipleship and the word process are rather synonymous. *They denote that time is required.* In other words, I have never seen a book entitled The Thirty Second Disciple of Christ. Maybe I will write that book next. The first sentence will have to explain that the title is completely misleading. It is obvious! There are no real disciples made in thirty seconds. It would be impossible!

> A patient person is one who having the resources and opportunity to avenge oneself, chooses to refrain from the exercise of these.
>
> *Chrysostom*

As I write today, I know that some of you are experiencing situations and circumstances that you would love to see changed. Let me encourage you not to jump on the first train out of Dodge! The quick or easy fix most often leaves you trying to repair the damage over and over again. In my personal yet valid experience, I try to allow God as much time as He needs to fix my situation because I took plenty of time getting myself into the *broken* situation. The Old Testament makes reference to the fact that God will restore all that the locusts have eaten. The word *restore* also denotes a process and the subsequent time required to complete the process. I've refinished enough furniture to know that. It would behoove us to give God as much time to restore our lives as we took in the ruination. *That's just my humble, but correct, opinion.*

Those who wait patiently on God will have their strength renewed and shall one day walk and run without the slightest fatigue; they shall even soar as eagles, lifted by the very winds that once fought against them.

Isaiah 40:31

Out Of My Way
Molasses Lady

I went to Lamaze Class with my wife; I think it really prepared me for that kidney stone I had to pass last summer.

Mike G. Williams

I have always had a love for speed. In fact, there is not much I do that is not done at full throttle. So when I took that ski lift up to the top of the Gatlinburg Mountain, I intended to have the race of my life. I only had a few minutes before I needed to get back to the conference, and I was really not properly attired to spend much time out in the blustery February weather The lady on the plastic wheeled bobsled in front of me explained that she would be going very slowly and to please not bump her. I thought, "Great, my one run and I'm behind a grandmother that thinks backing up is progress!" So when the gate attendant told her to go, I quickly started up a conversation with him to distract his normal pacing between sleds. "Where are you from? You don't seem to have an eastern Tennessee accent... blah, blah, blah. It has been a few years and a few pounds since I took this little bobsled ride for amateurs, it looks like they lengthened the run," I said questioningly. He replied, "Yes they did, and now it is *impossible* for the sleds to fly off the track." Well hearing something like that only makes a speed demon like myself feel as if there is another limit I don't have to concern

> If only God would give me some clear sign! Like making a large deposit in my name at a Swiss bank.
>
> *Woody Allen*

130

myself with pushing. I conversed long enough to gain a good two minutes between my sled and *Molasses Lady.*

I don't know if you have ever been on an alpine slide. It is a combination of bobsledding, skateboarding, and riding a little red wagon, all wrapped up in a little publicly insurable package. *You really need to try it sometime.* You sit on top of a scalloped plastic sled with four wheels protruding from the bottom. The brake is a simple center mounted stick which lifts the plastic sled up and down. The forward motion of this stick causes the sled to gain speed, whereas the pulling back of this stick causes the sled to slow down. I guess I should also mention that the track is a half-circle of concrete that winds its way down the side of a mountain.

The time had come for me to make my run. I was allowed to proceed down the track when I was ready, so with a hard forward thrust of the brake release/speed stick, I began to let gravity take my husky torso down the hill as my Olympic dreams ran wild with thoughts of gold. I truly expected the workers at the bottom to compliment my riding prowess and tell me that I was the fastest slider they had seen in years and ask me where I trained? *How silly our male ego's can be!*

As I came upon the first banked turn, my weight and the sled velocity put me high on the banked wall. Almost enough to make me back off the throttle, but no, I plowed on. *Hey, the cart "can't" come off the track anymore. I believe the track-master used the word "impossible!"* So with the nerves of the Jamaican Bobsled team, I shot down the concrete half pipe like gas through a funnel and eggs through a hen. *I guess you could also compare it to eggs going through a funnel and gas through a hen. There is not a huge difference.* I must have been going close to 50 mph as I reached the third and fourth hairpins. That was the moment I realized something was wrong. Maybe I misunderstood the "wording." *The sled cannot fly off the track; however, he never said that I, being a man whose mass was distributed quite plentifully above the center of gravity, was incapable of flying off the sled!* You guessed it! I didn't even see it coming. It was like a car crash! All I can remember is being tossed around and having my body thrown clear. I don't remember the EMT's getting

> The luge is one event that you could participate in on an involuntarily basis. Just grab a guy out of the crowd, slap a helmet on him, and throw him onto the icy track. There he goes! Instead of the Bobsled... the luge would simply be... Bob!
>
> *Jerry Seinfeld*

there either. I do remember the really fun high-speed ride down the mountain to the hospital. I was not in any kind of critical condition, but I think the driver apparently liked high speed driving as much as I do.

"The wording" is ever so important! Sometimes our misunderstanding can result in catastrophe! So what does this have to do with anything? I am saying that we need to read the fine print. It is so easy for our emotions, or our personality types to overlook obvious flaws in the safety systems of life. We forge ahead uninhibited, because we are assured that others have done it with great success. In Ephesians Chapter 5, we are given specific instruction as to the running of this course in life. We are asked to walk in love as Christ demonstrated. We are asked to beware of the fornication, uncleanness, and covetousness. They will throw us from the track. We are warned of the sharp curves of foolish talking, filthiness, and connections to evil people. These too will throw us from the intended course. It warns us of the dangers of excess that cause our sleds to be top heavy, and reminds us to be filled constantly, daily, moment-ly (I don't think that is a real word) with the Spirit of God. I certainly believe that God has some phenomenal EMT's, but obedience is always better than scar tissue.

> Success can only be measured by how well we meet the demands that God has put upon our life and how closely our life resembles that of Christ.
>
> *Mike G. Williams*

You see, the track that we are called to use is amazingly steep and extremely narrow at times. But the sled will not fly off the track! The sled will get us to the intended destination. We must let go of the excess that causes us to be out of sync with the sled. We must seek to discard that which makes us top heavy. I don't think I can explain this any more fully than that. *If you get it—you get it!* Let go of that which is pulling you from the destination. Let go of that which is slowing you down. Let go of the things that cause you to fear and doubt. Live with your grip firmly on the sled of the Spirit and have the ride of your life.

Excesses cause us to lose grip on our calling, beware of any kind of obesity; rather be filled daily and completely with the Spirit of God.
Ephesians 5:18

Curtain Call

Kids say the darndest things! And so would you if you had little education.

Eugene Mervin

*W*hen I was fourteen my father brought home a southern gospel record. I believe it was by the LeFevere's. Some of you may remember their once-wayward son Mylon, and his rise to fame in the contemporary Christian world. On dad's old, vinyl black disc were many great songs and an a musical poem. It was one of those emotional "Heaven Poems" for which the southern gospel genre of music is noted. In fact, I have often joked that if I ever heard a southern gospel song that wasn't about heaven, I would donate money to the *United Way. So far that organization has not made it to my yearly contribution list!* I have also offered to donate to a fund for people recovering from bad make-up and purple hair addiction. I guess I will save that for another chapter. Maybe I should get back to the poem. I have always been moved by words, so the honest southern accent and harmonious background singing hooked me like a big fish. To this day, I still love a good story song.

One Sunday morning as we motored toward the church, my dad mentioned that he liked that musical poem I mentioned earlier. Desirous of affirmation from my father, I quickly blasted into this four-minute (yes, I said four minute) poetic dissertation on heaven. Sitting rather erect I said, "When I picture heaven and quite often I do, I may not think of the things that mean most to me and you…" The poem went on to list the every conceivable, tangible joy of heaven, and just when you thought (or hoped) it was nearing the close, it turned to family. I rhymed, "Another thing to me will make heaven so fair, is my mom and dad will both be there, and looking so young and fair to see, not old and wrinkled like they used to be. I want to kiss mom and hear her whisper in my ear, I've been waiting for you son, I'm so glad you're here..." And then again, when you thought (or prayed) that it was finally the end of this emotional ride, the poem took another turn. "But the main thing that awaits us when we get up there will be to see Jesus, the one who died for me, and to live in His presence for all eternity..." And it went on from there. *It went on like the overly repeated reprise of the Hallelujah Chorus, as sung by Mrs. Rikers third grade class, all hopped-up on powdered sugar donuts only moments before the Kindergarten Easter Pageant.*

> Travel the path of integrity without looking back, because if you look back you may find that others are gaining on you and thus choose to be unscrupulous.
>
> *Mike G. Williams*

Admittedly, it was a great poem that still brings tears to my eyes, but it was longer than most people could stand. *Especially when delivered by a fourteen year old, who actually contemplated heaven or eternity about as much as a can of Spam would contemplate an expiration date.* Usually my parents would convince our Pastor to let me share it at church once a year. Of course, I had to deliver it at every single family gathering, while my aunts and uncles pretended that they had not heard it last year, or the year before, or the year before that. Can you picture a rather stout, pimply teenager wearing a purple and gray plaid suit, delivering such a conservative reprise? *Me either, at least not without laughing out loud, or choking on my artificially flavored raspberry quiche.* So I guess my foray into the comedy world is not that far fetched. I was making people laugh (at least internally) long before I ever took to the comedy stage for the first time at the age of thirty.

The world renowned Poet Philip Larkin commented on how that he *hated* live poetry readings, because he couldn't tell when the poem was going to end. He wanted to know when the end was near in order to, at very least, have time to prepare his emotions for the finish. He oft proclaimed that he loved poetry books because his eyes could scan the pages and see the finish was nearing. This gave him a visual precursor to the emotionally challenging conclusion. I have to admit that I can understand what he meant. In fact, I have been known to become so bored with a poem that I simply skipped ahead to the grand finale. I have done that with books also. I hope that is not the case for you. *If you are one of those people you may never even read these words. So, why am I addressing you?* I hope that these final paragraphs are the conclusion of many happy hours of reading. Or maybe I should say minutes, depending on your reading speed.

I believe most of us would like to know how our story will end, our story of life that is. It would be so much easier if we knew that we were going to live seventy years before we were called to stand before the Creator. It would allow us to prepare ourselves for the emotional adjustment. It would allow our family to prepare as well. Knowing our expiration date sure would seem like a good idea. Perhaps, a good idea until I really consider the ramifications.

First of all, I'm a procrastinator, which means that I would probably put off my eternal preparations until the night before. I was a "crammer" in high school and college, and I don't think I have changed all that much. I would probably put off the important things in light of the time I knew I was given. On the other hand, at my current age, if I knew I only had one more year, I would probably never go to work. I would spend the day hugging my family. *After about a month of my sloppy kissing and hugging, my family would be relieved to see me depart.* Maybe the surprise factor helps us be better mourners. I'm sure it will in my case.

Maybe it is best to have the *final curtain call* take us all by surprise. It causes us to live each and every day with a balance between the near and the far, between the playful and the inevitable. It causes us to serve God today with the fervor needed to stand before Him with a clear conscience tomorrow. It causes us to hold on a little longer to our spouses as we say goodbye each morning, but still get to work on time. It causes us to play a little more intently with our children as we invest time into their lives but still save for their college. It causes me to write words that are a little more pointed seeing that this very chapter may well be the last one I write. Yet I also know that this chapter could be merely the beginning of a long secession, which causes me to remain polite and uplifting in my wording. I can be rather crass and sarcastic at times. *But I'm sure you haven't noticed.*

> If there is no resurrection of the dead, than this life itself is an exercise in futility.
>
> *A*postle *P*aul
> paraphrased

135

As I wrap up this chapter by hitting the save button at the airport in Anchorage, Alaska, I say thanks. Thanks to you who have purchased this book and allowed me to make a decent living doing what I love. And I say thanks to my family for loving me unconditionally for many years. I must also say thanks to God the Father for sending His Son to give me eternal life, for He allows me to close this chapter with exuberant hope. Hope that says, "It isn't over for any of us, ever!" Yes, we have, through the gift of faith, the ability to look forward to the glorious future in a new world, an eternal world, a perfect place.

By the way, I'm ending now! I can only imagine what it will be like standing face to face with God. I wonder if I will cry, or dance, or fall to my knees. *Mercy me…someone ought to write a song about that.* I hope it's not a long one, and I hope that they tell us when the end of it is coming, so that we can emotionally adjust to the curtain call. I believe I will get my handkerchief out of my pocket now. But until that great day may you always remember: Life happens—shut up, laugh, and always carry a plunger! One more thing… enjoy the ride… it may be over before you think.

> The mountaintop/valley view of life is seriously flawed—it's one dimensional and inadequate. Now I believe roller coasters are a more accurate model of the Christian life. You say yes to Jesus, and suddenly you are strapped in and you think, *I'm going to die!* Then you began the long climb of growth—Sunday school, baptism, church membership—and you think, *Hey, no problem. I can follow Jesus anywhere,* and then—ZOOOOOM—you crash into the twists and turns of life, jerking left then right, up then down, and fifty, sixty years go by and—WHAM!—you're dead.
>
> *Michael Yaconelli*

Watch continually and be constantly prepared for we are clueless as to when we will have to stand before the Lord.
Matthew 25:13

The End

Other volumes of Turkey Soup for the Sarcastic Soul
are now available!

Please try and contain your excitement!

Complete your set today at

www.christiancomedian.com

PS: Order an extra copy for a friend,
I need the money, I want to buy a Jeep!